Bremen and Freiburg Lectures

Studies in Continental Thought

Martin Heidegger

Bremen and Freiburg Lectures

Insight Into That Which Is and
Basic Principles of Thinking

Translated by Andrew J. Mitchell

Indiana University Press
Bloomington and Indianapolis

This book is a publication of

Indiana University Press
601 North Morton Street
Bloomington, Indiana 47404-3797 USA

iupress.indiana.edu

Telephone orders   800-842-6796
Fax orders   812-855-7931

Published in German as Martin Heidegger,
Gesamtausgabe 79: Bremer und Freiburger Vorträge
Edited by Petra Jaeger
© 1994 by Vittorio Klostermann, Frankfurt am Main

♾ The paper used in this publication meets the minimum requirements of
the American National Standard for Information Sciences—Permanence of
Paper for Printed Library Materials, ANSI Z39.48-1992.

Manufactured in the United States of America

Library of Congress Cataloging-in-Publication Data

Heidegger, Martin, 1889–1976.
[Bremer und Freiburger Vorträge. English]
Bremen and Freiburg lectures : insight into that which is and basic principles
of thinking / Martin Heidegger ; translated by Andrew J. Mitchell.
p. cm. — (Studies in Continental thought)
ISBN 978-0-253-00231-0 (cloth : alk. paper) — ISBN 978-0-253-00716-2
(electronic book) 1. Knowledge, Theory of. 2. Ding an sich. 3. Thought and
thinking. 4. Reasoning. I. Title.
B3279.H48.B7413 2012
193—dc23

2012008012

1 2 3 4 5   17 16 15 14 13 12

CONTENTS

TRANSLATOR'S FOREWORD

This translation brings two key lecture cycles from Heidegger's later thinking to an English-language readership. Published as volume 79 of Heidegger's *Gesamtausgabe* (*Collected Edition*) in 1994, *Insight Into That Which Is* of 1949 is Heidegger's first speaking engagement after the Second World War, and *Basic Principles of Thinking* from 1957 is his last extended lecturing engagement at Freiburg University.[1] The texts taken together provide a panorama of the issues at stake in Heidegger's late thinking.

In many respects the Bremen lectures inaugurate the late period of Heidegger's thinking. It is here that he first formulates his conception of the thing as a gathering of the "fourfold" (*das Geviert*) and of technology as a matter of "positionality" (*das Gestell*). This basic tension in Heidegger's thought between a singular existence and the drive to replaceability is first articulated in these pages in a manner that is uncompromising if not, at times, shockingly blunt, especially in treating recent events from

---

1. Martin Heidegger, *Bremer und Freiburger Vorträge: 1. Einblick in Das Was Ist: Bremer Vorträge 1949, 2. Grundsätze des Denkens: Freiburger Vorträge 1957, Gesamtausgabe* vol. 79, ed. Petra Jaeger (Frankfurt am Main: Vittorio Klostermann, 1994). Volumes of Heidegger's *Gesamtausgabe* will henceforth be cited as "GA" by volume number, with first German then English pagination of available translations, separated by a slash. Heidegger's last teaching engagement at Freiburg was the 1966–67 *Heraclitus* seminar held with Eugen Fink. See Martin Heidegger and Eugen Fink, *Heraklit*, in Martin Heidegger, *Seminare*, GA 15, ed. Curd Ochwadt (Frankfurt am Main: Vittorio Klostermann, 1986), 9–266. English translation in Martin Heidegger and Eugen Fink, *Heraclitus Seminar*, trans. Charles H. Seibert (Evanston, Ill.: Northwestern University Press, 1993).

the war. In no uncertain terms, Heidegger announces the era of technological circulation to be a break with that of modern metaphysics and its conception of representational objectivity. The profundity of Heidegger's thinking, however, lies in his refusal to construe singularity and replacement as two separate orders of existence, but instead to understand them as mutually dependent upon each other. The thing needs the standing reserve to be what it is.

The 1957 Freiburg lectures, *Basic Principles of Thinking,* were the third and final installment in something of a trio of lecture courses Heidegger delivered in Freiburg on the topic of thinking (*What Is Called Thinking?* of 1951–52 and *The Principle of Reason* from 1955–56 being the earlier two). Here Heidegger traces the notions of being and thinking as operative in dialectical thought back to their roots in the Greek conception of the λόγος. From the Aristotelian conception of a λόγος ἀποφαντικός and its principle of grounding, however, Heidegger proposes a "leap into the abyss" whereby λόγος is understood more primordially (via Homer) as "saying" (*sagen*). Heidegger's concluding ruminations on the interconnection of being, language, and thinking are some of the most provocative of his career.

Both of these cycles taken together portray a world that is always arriving, a fragile world shadowed by danger, but a danger that likewise allows us to belong to that world. They present us with a vision of being as arriving, of things as dancing, and of language as an abyssal realm of appearing. Further details concerning the delivery of the lectures and the state of the manuscripts can be found in the German editor's afterword below (167–71).

A few of the translation choices in the lectures that follow warrant further explanation here. Additionally, full German-English and English-German glossaries are supplied after the main text. The following remarks sketch some of the conceptual considerations motivating the translations indicated, arranged here largely in order of appearance:

Das Geviert / the fourfold

The word names a gathering of four (earth, sky, divinities, mortals), the bringing together of four parties. How these elements hold together is articulated through the gathering power of the

German prefix *Ge-* (also to be heard in *Ge-Stell*, positionality, the gathering or collection of all puttings and placings, of modes of *stellen*). Nowhere is the operative force of this *Ge-* ever named a fold or folding. Of a literal "fourfold" (*Vierfalt*), Heidegger here does not speak. Thus, a neutral term like "foursome" would be preferable to "fourfold," which makes some unwarranted assumptions about the nature of the *Geviert*. Nevertheless, external considerations and unsavory associations lead to the retaining of "fourfold" to translate *Geviert*. To be sure, there is much mention of folding in the essay "The Thing," where the term *Geviert* first arises, but that is due to the repeated use of the term *Einfalt*. One must simply bear in mind that each of the four come together in a "single fold" and not in any multiplicity of folds as one might wrongly hear in the term "fourfold" (see GA 79: 12/11).

Die Einfalt / the single fold

The word identifies the simplicity of naivete, guilelessness. The *Einfalt* is not "complex," though the English language does not have a word like "uniplex," which is what the literal sense of the word leads us to think. It is the simplicity of a fold. Earlier translations elided the distinction between *Einfalt* and *Einfach* in Heidegger's work. Where the difference was remarked, it was often explained with the emphasis on the *Ein* as "simple oneness." This attributes too much weight to the unifying force of the *Ein*, while Heidegger's emphasis here falls much more on the "fold." The term itself emerges in the text in response to an act of folding: the four are "folded into a single fourfold [*in ein einziges Geviert eingefaltet*]" (GA 79: 12/11). The very next sentence then introduces the "single fold of the four [*die Einfalt der Vier*]" (GA 79: 12/11). This single fold names the simple belonging together of the four.

ring / nimble; scant
gering / lithe; slight

These terms are at the heart of Heidegger's conception of the "thinging" of the thing. Each presents two strands of meaning, with *gering* serving as an intensification of *ring* (according to the Grimms' *Deutsches Wörterbuch*). On the one hand, and as per Heidegger's own definition, the terms name the "supple,

lithesome, malleable, pliant, nimble" (see below, GA 79: 19/18).
On the other, they name the slight, scant, modest, and few. Heidegger uses both senses in his discussion, though the first more
positive sense predominates. In keeping with Heidegger's definitions, I have rendered *ring* as "nimble" and *gering* as "lithe"
when the emphasis is on the first sense. When the second sense
is operative, as in the closing passages of "The Thing," I have
rendered *ring* as "scant" and *gering* as "slight." Through these
terminological maneuvers, Heidegger seeks to avoid the Scylla
and Charybdis of construing the thing as either something sub-
stantial and solid or as something utterly diffuse or negligible.
The thinging of the thing does not take place in a second order
of reality apart from that of our own. These things are liminally
situated. Their nimbleness consists in their opening onto relations with the world around them via the mirror-play of the
fourfold. Neither present nor absent, things are "slightly" of the
world, we might say, and that is all they can ever be.

weilen / to abide
verweilen / to linger (intrans.); to let abide (trans.)

The thing abides (*weilt*). It remains for a while (*eine Weile*). This
"while" is the duration (*die Weile*) of that which abides (*ein
Weiliges*). Abiding is an open-ended lingering. There is a calm
to it (a *Ruhe* and a *Stille*), but it is a calm that is coterminous
with the shortness of one's stay. The difficulty for the translator here stems from Heidegger's use of the verb *verweilen* in a
transitive sense (previously translated as "to stay" or "to bring
to abide"). It names the way in which the fourfold coalesces in
the thinging of the thing. To capture this transitive sense, I
have sought to follow Heidegger's own indications from his
discussion some ten months later in the 1950 lecture "Language." Here the context is precisely that of the fourfold and
the thinging of the thing, with Heidegger stating that "the
things allow [*lassen*] the fourfold of the four to abide with
them [*bei sich verweilen*]. This gathering letting-abide [*Verwei-
lenlassen*] is the thinging of the thing."[2] Thus I have chosen to

2. Martin Heidegger, *Unterwegs zur Sprache, Gesamtausgabe* vol. 12, ed.
Friedrich-Wilhelm von Herrmann (Frankfurt a.M.: Vittorio Klostermann, 1985), 19. English translation: *Poetry, Language, Thought*, ed. and

follow Heidegger's own indication and render transitive uses of *verweilen* as "to let abide."

Das Ge-Stell / positionality
Die Gestelle / framework
Die Gestellung / conscription

Heidegger names the term *Ge-Stell* with the explicit intent of it expressing a gathering of some kind. It is the gathering of all *Stellen*, of all positioning, placing, putting as this basic movement has shown itself in the technologically dominated world of today as well as across the history of Western philosophy from its inception with the Greeks. Heidegger explicitly and painstakingly distinguishes what he means by positionality from any sense of "enframing" as the term has previously been translated. Positionality, Heidegger tells us, is not a frame like a bookcase that would contain its contents, nor is it like a water well that would surround its contents either (GA 79: 32/31). It is not even like a skeleton, a note to the manuscript informs us, that would structure its flesh from within (GA 79: 32n.j/32n. 10). This coarse sense of structure and framing is not to be heard in the term "positionality." Heidegger marks the difference himself when he explicitly distinguishes between positionality, *das Ge-Stell,* and framework, *die Gestelle* (GA 79: 65/61). The spread of positionality is thus not a framework that surrounds from without, but, in part, a process of conscription [*Gestellung*] that adopts and compels whatever it encounters into the order of standing reserve.

Einkehr / entrance

The turn of the *kehr* in *Ein-kehr* is not retained in the translation "entrance." Thus the reader must hear in the latter term a pivoting insurgence. Whatever enters with an *Einkehr* does not enter directly. There is a sweep to this entrance, it traces an arc, it is spaced. *Einkehr* is the way something enters that has been here all along, though inapparently, something like the forgetting of being, which makes its entrance and thereby becomes the guardianship of being. The *Einkehr* is the entrance that occurs

---

trans. Albert Hofstadter (New York: Perennial Classics, 2001), 197; translation modified.

with the turn that flips the forgetting of being into its preservation. Forgetting always harbored being, but this just needed to
make its entrance. A new face of things is revealed.

Die Verwindung / conversion

The term is presented as an alternative to the history of metaphysics and as a relationship to pain. We know from elsewhere
that it is precisely not a matter of "overcoming" (*Überwindung*)
that is at stake, but instead something else. In the *Verwindung*,
the prevailing situation (that which is) is seen in a flash to be
a dispensation of beyng, dislodging it of any presumed stabil-
ity. *Verwindung* can thus be heard as "bringing to a turning
point" or pivot point. It is the moment that the limit is achieved
and what once was construed as "inside" shows itself now as
exposed to an outside lying beyond it. One achieves a position
at the limit (of metaphysics, of beings, of being itself) around
which the whole will revolve. A new constellation becomes
visible now in a change of philosophical seasons. The perspective from the limit that is able to see how metaphysics is a
dispensation (i.e., is sent, has an outside) is now said to have
"converted" that former position. But just as a pain is converted into a part of one's identity through the formation of a
scar, so too are there traces of metaphysics to be found here as
well. There is no complete *Verwindung*, no final conversion, for
such would only be another "overcoming" (*Überwindung*), as
these are endemic to metaphysics. *Verwindung* in German car-
ries none of the religious overtones of "conversion" in English
(German, *Umkehrung*), but as the discussion is of lightning-
flash moments of the arrival of grace, these overtones are not
entirely foreign to the tenor of the text.

Gegen-wart / the impending

A proper understanding of this term is crucial for appreciating
Heidegger's conception of history and the "sending" of tempo-
rality. Heidegger is able to think the distance between the future and ourselves or the distance between what has-been and
ourselves as the distance necessary for an arrival. Both future
and what has-been arrive to us. We are exposed to their coming. But does this then mean that the present (*die Gegenwart*)
would simply be the site for their arrival? No. By *Gegen-wart,*

Heidegger now thinks the present itself as on the move. The present is nothing immediately present at our disposal. Instead, it waits for us, as the sense of *"warten"* in the word makes clear (and etymologically it is tied to keeping watch). Heidegger himself emphasizes that the *"gegen"* here is not to be understood as an "over against" as per modern metaphysics, but instead as an *"entgegen,"* a "toward." The *gegen* of *Gegenwart* is a directional term specifying the way in which the present that waits leans toward us or is inclining itself to us. The present is not present, but something that slants toward us, that is impending. The present, too, arrives.

Die Sage / the saying

The Grimms' *Deutsches Wörterbuch* mentions that *die Sage* indicates the spoken telling of history as opposed to the sung. Heidegger continues this thought in linking it to the Norse sagas via the Old High German term *sagan*, the art of the storyteller. It is something said, not spoken. Heidegger himself calls explicit attention to how he is using the term when he discusses it in conjunction with fairy tales and fables (GA 79: 170/160). The saying is what is truly fabulous. It is a different way of telling a history, of relaying a sending. It is "legendary." The saying is the realm (*Be-reich*) through which all such stories can reach us, speak to us—indeed it is the realm for any such reaching at all. It makes possible the relations, both disclosive and concealing, that are achieved through reaching. It is the medium that allows for reaching and stretching, which is to say, the saying is the medium of communication itself. The storyteller's saga is historical and heroic, the saying is the medium for this streaking afterglow.

ereignen (sich) / to take place

The event (*das Ereignis*) takes place (*ereignet sich*). The translation "to take place" draws attention to the spacing of the event of appropriation itself. What takes place is the thinging of the thing and the worlding of the world. What takes place is the belonging together of the human and being. Appropriation takes place. But insofar as all appropriating establishes a relationship between the parties involved, there is consequently a spacing to appropriation, a separation that is at once the space of their relating.

The event of appropriation is a spacing of things. If things themselves can be considered places, then in the taking place of the thinging of the thing, there is an emergence of place. Where *Ereignis* is a relation that is both given and taken up (see *vereignen* and *zueignen* below), then it is literally a taking (giving) of place. The locution "to take place" is used solely to translate *sich ereignen*.

vereignen / to deliver into the ownership of
zueignen / to take into ownership

These two terms express the transitivity of the event of appropriation (*Ereignis*). What is given or delivered into ownership is now owned by another. And what is so owned needs this other to be itself. But what gives or delivers into ownership is just as much owned in this relationship as is that which is given or delivered into the ownership of another (and beyng is the most other other because most near). What it is that is given over into the ownership of another here is one's very ownness as such. One's ownness is delivered to be taken up; never is even ownership simply one's own. In "The Thing," Heidegger will discuss this as a "mirroring" relation. Heidegger's language sets ownness into motion, given to one from what is not oneself, taken by one as part of oneself. The bond between oneself and another is negotiated in the terms *vereignen* and *zueignen*, giving and taking into ownership.

Within the text, my editorial interventions stand within square brackets. Heidegger's own insertions, as well as those of his German editor, stand within guillemets. In the interest of readability, Heidegger's hyphenation of terms—i.e. *Er-eignis*, *Unter-Schied*, etc.—has not always been retained in the text. Where such hyphenation emphasizes the force of the prefix at issue, I have supplied the German term in brackets at its first occurrence in the relevant discussion. In some instances, where the hyphenation draws attention to a literal meaning, I have provided the hyphenated term with its own distinct translation (*Gegenwart* = "present," but *Gegen-wart* = "the impending"). Capitalization of Greek text reproduces Heidegger's own usage (which does not simply follow the German practice of capitalizing all nouns).

The German edition of this volume contains two kinds of notes, notes to the text (identified by Arabic numerals and stemming from either Heidegger or, where indicated, his German editor) and Heidegger's handwritten marginal notes (identified by letters). All the textual notes are bibliographic and all the marginal notes but one are expansions on the text. The sole exception, which I have duly noted in the text, is note 16 in *Basic Principles of Thinking,* lecture 5, which is a marginal note from Heidegger supplying a bibliographic reference (to "Kant's Thesis About Being"). Thus it is easy to distinguish between text notes and marginal notes by content, and a single order of notes in Arabic numerals has been adopted in this translation. Consequently, apart from the sole exception just mentioned, where a bibliographic reference is supplied in the notes to this translation it corresponds to a textual note in the German edition (unless specifically indicated as a translator's note), and all other notes are Heidegger's marginal notes in the German text.

Heidegger's occasional parenthetical citations have been moved into the notes for greater consistency. Original bibliographic information for Heidegger's textual citations has been retained, but for ease of location these have been augmented with corresponding references to contemporary authoritative German editions of the texts in question. I have also supplied pagination for English translations immediately following these references. References to contemporary German editions and to all English editions are thus my own. Translator's notes are identified as such and largely supply bibliographic information for citations originally unsourced in the text.

As a final note on the translation, Heidegger's title for the second lecture cycle, *Basic Principles of Thinking,* reads in German *Grundsätze des Denkens,* where the genitive "of" is indicated in German by the definite article, something missing in an English translation. Thus Heidegger's worries over the hegemony of "the" thinking make far more sense in German than they do in English, where no definite article is present in the title. To remedy this, I have rendered Heidegger's emphasis upon *"das" Denken* as a concern with "thinking 'as such.'" All uses of the "as such" in this regard are of my own importing.

Lastly, for complete correspondence with the *Gesamtausgabe* text it is to be noted that the present translation silently includes the following slight adjustments (page numbers are to GA 79):

17	for "nähernd" read "nährend"
22	for "Füge der Seyns" read "Füge des Seyns"
28 n. d	for "Werk" read "Wort"
29 n. e	for "ἀλήθεια" read "ἀλήθεια"
87	for "vor der Verwüstung" read "von der Verwüstung"
87 n. 4	for "IV. Band" read "VI. Band"
99 n. 2	for "Die stille Stunde" read "Die stillste Stunde"
130 n. 1	for "1900" read "1901"
170	for "nicht nicht" read "sind nicht"
179	for "Physiotherapie" read "Psychotherapie"
179	for "Zuatz" read "Zusatz"

ACKNOWLEDGMENTS

My first thanks go to Amy Alexander for her unwavering encouragement during the course of this translation. I am especially grateful to Dee Mortensen, Janet Rabinowitch, and John Sallis at Indiana University Press for their patience, indulgence, and support. This volume has also benefited from the scrupulous attention of Jerome Veith, who served as reader of this translation for the press. Work on this translation was funded in part by a National Endowment for the Humanities Fellowship in the fall of 2009, and I am appreciative and honored to have received their assistance. I would like to thank Professor Malek Moazzam-Doulat (Occidental College) and Professor John Sallis (Boston College) for teaching earlier drafts of the Bremen lectures in their courses at the undergraduate and graduate level respectively. I would also like to express my gratitude to the students in my graduate seminar "Introduction to Late Heidegger" at Emory University, fall 2010, for their helpful comments and suggestions across the entire volume. Lastly, this translation could not have been completed without the unrelenting assistance of Dr. Peter Trawny, whose knowledge of Heidegger and sensitivity to his language knows no bounds and who was always available to answer grammatical, textual, and philosophical questions about these lectures, from the insignificant to the profound. The work is vastly improved thanks to all these people.

In translating these cycles, I have benefited from the work of translators before me who brought into English later essay versions of some of the lectures presented in the pages that follow. For *Insight Into That Which Is,* a later version of "The Thing" was translated by Albert Hofstadter in *Poetry, Language, Thought* (New York: Harper & Row, 1971), 165–82; portions of "Positionality" and the essay version of "The Turn" were first translated by William Lovitt in *The Question Concerning Technology and Other Essays* (New York: Harper & Row, 1977), 3–35, 36–49. The first lecture in *Basic Principles of Thinking*, published separately in 1958 under this same title, was translated by James G. Hart and John C. Maraldo in *The Piety of Thinking* (Bloomington: Indiana University Press, 1976), 46–58; a later essay version of the third lecture, "The Principle of Identity," was translated by Joan Stambaugh in *Identity and Difference* (New York: Harper & Row, 1969), 23–41. The clarity, elegance, and simplicity of their translation choices were often inspirations in the course of this work.

This translation is dedicated to William H. Bossart (Professor Emeritus, University of California Davis), who first introduced me to Heidegger.

Atlanta, May 2012
Andrew J. Mitchell

Bremen and Freiburg Lectures

INSIGHT INTO THAT WHICH IS:
BREMEN LECTURES 1949

The Point of Reference

All distances in time and space are shrinking. Places that a person previously reached after weeks and months on the road are now reached by airplane overnight. What a person previously received news of only after years, if at all, is now experienced hourly over the radio in no time. The germination and flourishing of plants that remained concealed through the seasons, film now exhibits publicly in a single minute. Film shows the distant cities of the most ancient cultures as if they stood at this very moment amidst today's street traffic. Beyond this, film further attests to what it shows by simultaneously displaying the recording apparatus itself at work along with the humans who serve it. The pinnacle of all such removals of distance is achieved by television, which will soon race through and dominate the entire scaffolding and commotion of commerce.

The human puts the longest stretches behind himself in the shortest time. He puts the greatest distances behind him and thus puts everything at the shortest distance before him.

Yet the hasty setting aside of all distances brings no nearness; for nearness does not consist in a small amount of distance. What confronts us at the shortest distance in terms of length, through the imagery of film or the sound of the radio, can remain remote to us. What is vastly far away in terms of length, can be near to us. Short distance is not already nearness. Great distance is not yet remoteness.

What is nearness if it remains outstanding despite the shrinking of the greatest lengths to the shortest distances? What is nearness if it is even warded off by the restless removal

3

of distances? What is nearness when, along with its own exclusion, remoteness too remains away?

What is happening when, through the removal of great distances, everything stands equally near and far? What is this uniformity wherein everything is neither far nor near and, as it were, without distance?

Everything washes together into the uniformly distanceless. How? Is not this moving together into the distanceless even more uncanny than everything being out of place? The human is transfixed by what could come about with the explosion of the atomic bomb. The human does not see what for a long time now *has* already arrived and even *is* occurring, and for which the atomic bomb and its explosion are merely the latest emission, not to speak of the hydrogen bomb, whose detonation, thought in its broadest possibility, could be enough to wipe out all life on earth. What is this clueless anxiety waiting for, if the horrible [*das Entsetzliche*] *has* already occurred?

The horrifying is what transposes [*heraussetzt*] all that is out of its previous essence. What is so horrifying? It reveals and conceals itself in the way that everything presences, namely that despite all overcoming of distance, the nearness of that which is remains outstanding.

The Thing

How do things stand with nearness? How can we experience its essence? Nearness, it seems, cannot be immediately found. We sooner achieve this by pursuing what is in the vicinity [*in der Nähe*]. In the vicinity are what we customarily name "things." But what is a thing? How long has the human observed and questioned things, how variously has he used them and, indeed, even used them up. And guided by such intentions, how insistently has he also explained the things, that is, led them back to their causes. The human has proceeded in this manner with things for a long time, and he is even still so proceeding, without ever once in all this considering the thing *as thing*.

Up to now, the human has considered the thing as a thing just as little as he has considered nearness. The jug is a thing. What is a jug? We say: a vessel; that which holds another in itself. What does the holding in the jug are the base and sides. This holding itself can be held at the handle. As a vessel, the jug is something that stands on its own. This standing-on-its-own characterizes the jug as something independent. As the self-standing [*Selbststand*] of something independent, the jug is distinguished from an object [*Gegenstand*]. Something independent can become an object when we represent it to ourselves, be it in immediate perception, be it in a thoughtful remembrance that makes it present. The thinghood of the thing, however, does not reside in the thing becoming the object of a representation, nor can the thinghood of the thing at all be determined by the objectivity of the object, not even when we take the opposition of the object as not simply due to our representation, but rather leave opposition to the object itself as its own affair.

5

The jug remains a vessel, whether we represent it or not. As a vessel, the jug stands on its own. But what does this mean, that what holds would stand on its own? Does the standing-on-its-own of the vessel already define the jug as a thing? To be sure, the jug stands as a vessel only insofar as it was brought to a stand. Of course this occurred, and it does so occur, through a posing [*ein Stellen*], namely through a producing [*das Herstellen*]. The potter completes the earthen jug from out of the earth that has been especially selected and prepared for it. The jug consists of this. By virtue of what it consists of, the jug is also able to stand upon the earth, be it directly, be it indirectly upon a table and bench. What subsists through such production is what stands on its own. If we take the jug to be a produced vessel then it indeed appears that we grasp it as a thing and by no means as a mere object.

Or do we even now still take the jug as an object? Just so. To be sure, it no longer counts as solely the object of a mere representation, but it is the object that a producing delivers and puts here, placing it against us and across from us. Standing-on-its-own seemed to characterize the jug as a thing. In truth, we nevertheless think this standing-on-its-own in terms of production. Standing-on-its-own is that toward which producing is directed. Standing-on-its-own is therefore still thought, and despite everything is ever still thought, in terms of an objectivity, even if the objective-stance of what is produced is no longer grounded in a mere representing. Indeed, from the objectivity of the object and the objectivity of what is self-standing, no road leads to the thinghood of the thing.

What is it that is thing-like in the thing? What is the thing in itself? We only arrive at the thing in itself if our thinking has previously reached the thing as thing.

The jug is a thing as a vessel. To be sure, this holder requires a producing. But the production by the potter by no means constitutes what is proper to the jug insofar as it is a jug. The jug is not a vessel because it was produced, rather the thing must be produced because it is this vessel.

The producing lets the jug freely enter into its own. Yet the essence of the jug's own is never completed by a producing. Let loose through its completion, the jug gathers itself in what is its own so as to hold. In the process of production, however, the jug must show its outward appearance to the producer beforehand. But this self-showing, this outward appearing (the εἶδος, the ἰδέα), characterizes the jug solely in the respect that the vessel stands across from the production as something to be set here.

What the vessel in this outward appearing is as jug, what and how the jug is as this jug-thing, can never be experienced, much less appropriately thought, with regard to the outward appearance, the ἰδέα. For this reason, Plato, who represented the presence of what is present on the basis of the outward appearance, thought the essence of things as little as Aristotle and all subsequent thinkers. Setting the standard for what was to come, Plato had much more experienced all presencing as the object of a producer; instead of object [Gegenstand], we say more precisely: what stands here [Herstand]. In the full essence of what stands here, a twofold standing-here holds sway; on the one hand, standing in the sense of a stemming from . . . , be this a bringing forth of oneself or a being produced; on the other hand, a standing here in the sense where what is brought forth stands here in the unconcealment of what is already presencing.

All representing of what presences in the sense of something standing here and of something objective, however, never reaches the thing as thing. The thinghood of the jug lies in that it is as a vessel. We become aware of what does the holding in the vessel when we fill the jug. The base and siding obviously take over the holding. But not so fast! When we fill the jug with wine, do we pour the wine into the sides and base? We pour the wine at most between the sides and upon the base. Sides and base are indeed what is impermeable in the vessel. But the impermeable is not yet what holds. When we fill up the jug, in the filling, the pour flows into the empty jug. The empty is what holds in the vessel. The empty, this nothing in the jug, is what the jug is as a holding vessel.

Yet the jug does consist of sides and base. By virtue of what the jug consists of, it stands. What would a jug be if it did not stand? At the very least a failed jug; and therefore always still a jug, namely one that indeed would hold, but as constantly toppling over it is a vessel that spills. But only a vessel can spill.

The sides and the base, of which the jug consists and by which it stands, are not what properly do the holding. But if this lies in the emptiness of the jug, then the potter, who shapes the sides and base upon the potter's wheel, does not actually finish the jug. He only forms the clay. No—he forms the emptiness. For this emptiness, within it, and from out of it, he shapes the clay into a figure. The potter grasps first and constantly what is ungraspable in the empty and produces it as what holds in the form of a vessel. The empty of the jug determines every grip of the production. The thinghood of the vessel by no means rests in the material of which it consists, but instead in the emptiness that holds.

But is the jug really empty?

The physical sciences assure us that the jug is filled with air and with all that constitutes the compound mixture of air. We let ourselves be deceived by a semipoetic manner of observation in calling upon the emptiness of the jug.

But as soon as we leave this aside so as to investigate the actual jug scientifically and in regards to its actuality, then another state of affairs shows itself. If we pour wine into the jug we merely force out the air that already fills the jug and replace it with a fluid. Viewed scientifically, to fill the jug means to exchange one filling for another.

These suppositions of physics are correct. By means of them science represents something actual, according to which it objectively judges. But—is this actual something the jug? No. Science only ever encounters that which its manner of representation has previously admitted as a possible object for itself.

It is said that the knowledge of science is compelling. Certainly. But what does its compulsion consist of? In our case, in the compulsion to relinquish the jug filled with wine and to put in its place a cavity in which a fluid expands. Science makes the jug-thing into something negligible, insofar as the thing is not admitted as the standard.

Within its purview, that of objects, the compelling knowledge of science has already annihilated the thing as thing long before the atomic bomb exploded. The explosion of the atomic bomb is only the crudest of all crude confirmations of an annihilation of things that occurred long ago: confirmation that the thing as thing remains nullified. The annihilation is so uncanny because it brings with it a twofold delusion. For one, the opinion that science, more so than all other experience, would encounter the actual in its actuality. Second, the pretense that the thing could just as well be a thing regardless of scientific research into the actual, which presupposes that there ever were essencing things at all. If the things had ever shown themselves as things, then the thinghood of the thing would have been evident. It would have laid claim to thinking. In truth, however, the thing remains obstructed as thing, nullified and in this sense annihilated. This occurred and occurs so essentially that the things are not only no longer admitted as things, but the things have not yet ever been able to appear as things at all.

What is the basis for the non-appearing of the thing as thing? Has the human simply neglected to represent the thing as thing? The human can only neglect what has already been allotted him. The human can represent, regardless of the manner, only that which has first lit itself up from itself and shown itself to him in the light that it brings with it.

But what now is the thing as thing such that its essence has never been able to appear?

Did the thing never come into the nearness enough such that the human could adequately learn to attend to the thing as thing? What is nearness? We asked this already. We asked in order to experience the jug in the vicinity.

What is the jughood of the jug? We have suddenly lost it from view and indeed at the very moment of intrusion by the pretense that science would be able to provide us with information as to the actuality of the actual jug.

We represented what is effective of the vessel, its holding—the empty—as a cavity filled with air. This is the empty thought as actual, in terms of physics, but it is not the empty of the jug. We do not let the empty of the jug be its empty. We did not attend to what does the holding in the vessel. We did not consider how the holding itself essences. For this reason, what the jug holds must also escape us. Wine becomes for the scientific representation a mere liquid, a universally possible aggregate state of matter. We left off considering what the jug holds and how it holds.

How does the empty of the jug hold? It holds in that it takes what is poured into it. It holds in that it retains what is taken up. The empty holds in a twofold manner: taking and retaining. The word "holding" is thus ambiguous. The taking of what is poured in and the retaining of the pour nevertheless belong

together. Their unity, however, is determined by the pouring
out, to which the jug as jug is correlated. The twofold holding of
the empty consequently lies in the outpouring. As this, the
holding is authentically how it is. The outpour from out of the
jug is a giving [*Schenken*]. In the gift of the pour there essences
the holding of the vessel. This holding requires the empty as
what holds. The essence of the holding empty is gathered in the
giving. Giving, however, is richer than a mere outpouring. The
giving, whereby the jug is a jug, gathers in itself the twofold
holding and does so in the outpouring. We name the collection
of mountains [*der Berge*] a mountain range [*das Gebirge*]. We
name the collection of the twofold holding in the outpouring,
which together first constitutes the full essence of giving [*des
Schenkens*]: the gift [*das Geschenk*]. The jughood of the jug essences in the gift of the pour. Even the empty jug retains its
essence from out of the gift, even if an empty jug is not capable
of an outpouring. But this "not capable" is appropriate to the
jug and to the jug alone. A scythe, on the contrary, or a ham-
mer are incapable of achieving the "not capable" of this gift.

The gift of the pour can be a libation. There is water, there
is wine to drink.[1]   *for mortals*

In the water of the gift there abides the spring. In the spring
abides the stone and all the dark slumber of the earth, which
receives the rain and dew of the sky. In the water of the spring
there abides the marriage of sky and earth. They abide in the
wine that the fruit of the vine provides, in which the

---

1. Addendum to manuscript page 9:

How does the empty of the jug hold? It takes up what is poured in, in
order to preserve it for an outpouring. The empty takes the pour and
gives it to such a pouring. The kind of pour makes an impression upon
the emptiness of the jug. The pour determines the jughood of the jug.
What is authentic of the pour is nevertheless the outpouring. It brings
the pour either into a drinking vessel or the pour can be immediately
drunk in the outpouring of the jug. The pour of the jug is a libation.
Every libation out of the jug is a pour. But not every pour of the jug is a
libation. This holds precisely for the authentic pour, which in its outpouring is indeed squandered, but not drunk.

Even the emptiness of the jug remains determined by the pour and in
relation to it. The pour can be a libation, insofar as the pour is water or
wine.

nourishment of the earth and the sun of the sky are betrothed to each other. In the gift of water, in the gift of wine, there abides in each case the sky and earth. The gift of the pour however is the jughood of the jug. In the essence of the jug there abides earth and sky.

The gift of the pour is a libation for the mortals. It quenches their thirst. It enlivens their efforts. It heightens their sociability. But the gift of the jug is also at times given for consecration. If the pour is for consecration then it does not appease a thirst. It appeases the celebration of the festival on high. Now the gift of the pour is neither given in a tavern nor is the gift a libation for mortals. The pour is the oblation spent for the immortal gods. The gift of the pour as oblation is the authentic gift. In the giving of the consecrated oblation, the pouring jug essences as the giving gift. The consecrated oblation is what the word "pour" actually names: offering and sacrifice. "Pour" [*Guß*], "to pour" [*gießen*], in Greek reads: χέειν, Indogermanic: *ghu*. This means: to sacrifice. Sufficiently thought and genuinely said, where it is essentially performed pouring is: donating, sacrificing, and therefore giving. Only for this reason can pouring become, as soon as its essence atrophies, a mere filling up and emptying out, until it finally degenerates into the ordinary serving of drinks. Pouring is not a mere gushing in and out.

In the gift of the pour that is a libation, the mortals abide in their way. In the gift of the pour that is an oblation, the divinities abide in their way, divinities who receive back the gift of the giving as the gift of a donation. In the gift of the pour, the mortals and divinities each abide differently. In the gift of the pour, the earth and sky abide. In the gift of the pour there abides at the same time earth and sky, divinities and mortals. These four, united of themselves, belong together. Obligingly coming before all that presences, they are folded into a single fourfold.

In the gift of the pour abides the single fold [*Einfalt*] of the four.

The gift of the pour is a gift insofar as it lets the earth and sky, the divinities and mortals abide. Indeed letting abide [*verweilen*] is now no longer the mere perseverance of something present at hand. Letting abide appropriates. It brings the four into the light of what is their own. From the single fold of this, they are entrusted to each other. At one in this reciprocality they are unconcealed. The gift of the pour lets the single fold of the fourfold of the four abide. In the gift, however, the jug essences as jug. The gift gathers that which belongs to giving: the twofold holding, the holder, the empty, and the outpouring as donating. What is gathered in the gift appropriatingly gathers itself therein so as to let the fourfold abide. This manifold and simplistic gathering is the essencing of the jug. Our language names what gathering is with an old word. It reads: *thing* [thing]. The essence of the jug exists as the pure giving gathering of the simple fourfold in a while [*eine Weile*]. The jug essences as thing. The jug is the jug as a thing. But how does the thing essence? The thing things. Thinging gathers. Appropriating the fourfold, it gathers the fourfold's duration [*dessen Weile*] each time into something that abides [*je Weiliges*]: into this or that thing.

We give to the essence of the jug, so experienced and thought, the name thing. We think this name in terms of the issue at stake for the thing, from thinging as the gathering-appropriative letting abide of the fourfold. We recall, however, at the same time the Old High German word *thing*. This linguistic historical reference easily seduces one to misunderstand the way we now think the essence of the thing. It might appear as if the essence of the thing now intended was whimsically spun, so to speak, from randomly snatched-up definitions of the Old High German noun *thing*. The suspicion arises that the experience of the essence of the thing now attempted would be grounded on the arbitrarity of an etymological game. The opinion calcifies and even becomes commonplace that here instead of considering the matter at stake, the dictionary alone would be deployed.

Indeed the opposite of such fears is the case. The Old High German word *thing* means gathering and indeed a gathering for the negotiation of an affair under discussion, a disputed case. Consequently the Old High German words *thing* and *dinc* become the name for an affair; they name what concernfully approaches the human in some way, what accordingly is under discussion. What is under discussion the Romans name *res;* ῥέειν, ῥῆμα, means in Greek: to speak about something, to negotiate about it; *res publica* does not mean: the state, but rather that which openly concerns every one of the people and therefore is negotiated publicly.

Only because *res* signifies what concernfully approaches can it lead to the compound words *res adversae, res secundae;* the former is that which concernfully approaches the human in an adverse way, the latter what favorably accompanies the human. The dictionary, however, translates *res adversae* with misfortune, *res secundae* with luck; of that which the words say when spoken as they are thought, the dictionaries say nothing. In truth, here and in the rest of the cases it is not that our thinking lives off etymology, but rather that etymology along with the dictionaries still think too little.

The Roman word *res* names that which concernfully approaches the human, the affair, the disputed matter, the case. For this the Romans also used the word *causa.* In no way does this authentically and primarily mean "cause"; *causa* means "the case" and for this reason also "that which is the case," that something comes to pass and becomes due. Only because *causa,* nearly synonymous with *res,* means the case can the word *causa* subsequently attain the meaning of cause in the sense of the causality of an effect. The Old High German word *thing* or *dinc,* with its meaning of gathering, namely for the negotiation of an affair, is thus appropriate like no other for fittingly translating the Roman word *res,* that which concernfully approaches. But from this word of the Roman language, with its inner correspondence to the word *res,*[2] from the word *causa* in the meaning of case and affair, there arose in the Romance languages *la cosa* and the French *la chose;* we say: *das Ding.* In English, *thing* still has retained the robust naming power of the Roman word *res: he knows his things,* he has an understanding of his "affair," of that which concerns him; *he knows how to handle things,* he knows how one must proceed with matters, i.e., what it concerns from case to case; *that's a great thing:* that is a great (fine, powerful, splendid) matter, i.e., something that comes of its own accord to the human in a concernful approach.[3]

Yet what is decisive is by no means the semantic history of the words briefly mentioned here: *res, Ding, causa, cosa* and *chose, thing,* but rather something entirely different and hitherto not at

---

2. at the earliest

3. Translator's Note: italicized phrases here in English in the original.

all considered. The Roman word *res* names that which in some way concernfully approaches the human. What concernfully approaches is the *reale* of the *res*. The *realitas* of the *res* was experienced by the Romans as what concernfully approached. But the Romans have never properly thought what they thus experienced in its essence. Much more, through the adoption of late Greek philosophy, the Roman *realitas* of the *res* was conceived in the sense of the Greek ὄν; now ὄν, Latin *ens*, means what presences in the sense of what stands here. The *res* becomes *ens*, that which presences in the sense of what is produced and represented. The characteristic *realitas* of the originally Roman experienced *res*, the concernful approach, remains buried as the essence of what presences. Conversely, in subsequent times, particularly the Middle Ages, the name *res* serves to indicate every *ens qua ens*, i.e., everything that is somehow presencing, even if it only stands here in representation and presences like the *ens rationis*. The same thing that happens with the word *res* happens with the name corresponding to *res*, *dinc*; for *dinc* means every single thing that somehow is. Accordingly Meister Eckhart uses the word *dinc* as much for God as for the soul. God is to him the "highest and most elevated thing [*dinc*]."⁴ The soul is a "great thing [*dinc*]."⁵ With this, this Master of thinking by no means wishes to say that God and the soul would be the same as a block of stone, a material object; *dinc* is here the careful and unassuming name for anything that is at all. Thus Meister Eckhart, following a saying of Dionysius the Areopagite <Ed.: Augustine is

---

4. Meister Eckhart, Sermon LI, in: *Deutsche Mystiker des vierzehnten Jahrhunderts,* vol. 2: *Meister Eckhart,* ed. Franz Pfeiffer (Leipzig: G. J. Göschen'sche Verlagshandlung, 1857; reprint, Aalen, Germany: Scientia Verlag, 1962), 168–70, 169. Now Predigt 100, *Die deutschen Werke,* vol. 4.1: *Meister Eckharts Predigten,* ed. and trans. Georg Steer with Wolfgang Klimanek and Freimut Löser (Stuttgart: Kohlhammer, 2003), 271–78, 275. English translation: Sermon 51, *Meister Eckhart by Franz Pfeiffer,* ed. and trans. C. de B. Evans (London: John M. Watkins, 1924), 132–34, 133.

5. Meister Eckhart, Sermon XLII, *Deutsche Mystiker,* 140–45, 141. Now Predigt 69, *Die deutschen Werke,* vol. 3: *Meister Eckharts Predigten,* ed. and trans. Josef Quint (Stuttgart: Kohlhammer, 1976), 159–80, 164. English translation: Sermon 42, *The Complete Mystical Works of Meister Eckhart,* ed. and trans. Maurice O'C. Walshe, rev. Bernard McGinn (New York: Crossroad Publishing, 2009), 233–37, 234.

probably meant>, says: love is of such a nature that it changes man into the things [*dink*] he loves.[6]

Because the word "thing" in the language use of Western metaphysics names something that is in any way at all, the meaning of the noun "thing" changes according to the interpretation of that which is, i.e., of beings. Kant speaks of things in the same manner as Meister Eckhart and means with this term something that is. But for Kant, that which is becomes the object of a representing that terminates in the self-consciousness of the human I. The thing in itself means for Kant: the object [*Gegenstand*] in itself. The character of the "in itself" means for Kant that the object in itself is an object without relation to human representation, i.e., without that "against" [*Gegen*] by means of which it stands for this representing in the first place. Thought in a rigorously Kantian manner, "thing in itself" means an object that is not an object, because it is supposed to stand without a possible "against" for the human representing that comes across it.

Neither the long-used-up general meaning of the noun "thing" as employed in philosophy, nor the Old High German meaning of the word *thing*, however, help us in the least in our predicament of experiencing and sufficiently thinking the factual essence of what we now say concerning the essence of the jug. Against this, however, one aspect of meaning from the old linguistic usage of the word "thing" does address the essence of the jug as thought here, namely that of "gathering."

The jug is a thing, neither in the sense of the *res* as meant by the Romans, nor in the sense of the *ens* conceived in the Middle Ages, nor even in the sense of the object of modern representation. The jug is a thing not as object, whether this be one of production or of mere representation. The jug is a thing insofar as it things. From the thinging of the thing there

---

6. cf. Meister Eckhart, Sermon LXIII, *Deutsche Mystiker*, 197–99, 199. Now Predigt 40, *Die deutschen Werke*, vol. 2: *Meister Eckharts Predigten*, ed. and trans. Josef Quint (Stuttgart: Kohlhammer, 1971), 271–81, 277–78, and Sermon XX, *Deutsche Mystiker*, 85–88, 86. Now Predigt 44, *Die deutschen Werke*, vol. 2, 337–51, 343. English translation: Eckhart, *Complete Mystical Works*, Sermon 63, 318–21, 320, and Sermon 20, 143–47, 144–45.

takes place and is first determined the presencing of what presences after the manner of the jug.

Today everything that presences is equally near and far. The distanceless dominates. All shortening and abolition of distances, however, brings no nearness. What is nearness? To find the essence of nearness, we considered a jug in the vicinity. We sought the essence of nearness and found the essence of the jug as thing. With this finding, however, we simultaneously become aware of the essence of nearness. The thing things. By thinging it lets the earth and sky, divinities and mortals abide. By letting abide, the thing brings the four in their remoteness near to each other. This bringing near is nearing. Nearing is the essence of nearness. Nearness brings near what is far off and indeed as the far-off. Nearness guards what is remote. Guarding remoteness, nearness essences in its nearing. Nearing in such a manner, nearness conceals itself and remains in its way what is most near.

The thing is not "in" the vicinity as though this would be a container. Nearness reigns in nearing as the thinging of the thing.

By thinging, the thing lets the united four, earth and sky, divinities and mortals, abide in the single fold of their fourfold, united of themselves.

The earth is the building bearer, what nourishingly fructifies, tending waters and stones, plants and animals.

When we say earth then we already think, in case we are thinking, the other three along with it from the single fold of the fourfold.

The sky is the path of the sun, the course of the moon, the gleam of the stars, the seasons of the year, the light and twilight of day, the dark and bright of the night, the favor and inclemency of the weather, drifting clouds, and blue depths of the ether.

When we say sky then we already think, in case we are thinking, the other three along with it from the single fold of the four.

The divinities are the hinting messengers of godhood. From the concealed reign of these there appears the god in his essence, withdrawing him from every comparison with what is present.

When we name the divinities then we already think, in case we are thinking, the other three along with them from the single fold of the four.

The mortals are the humans. They are called the mortals because they are able to die. Dying means: to be capable of death as death. Only the human dies. The animal comes to an end. It has death as death neither before it nor after it. Death is the shrine of the nothing, namely of that which in all respects is never some mere being, but nonetheless essences, namely as being itself. Death, as the shrine of nothing, harbors in itself what essences of being. As the shrine of the nothing, death is the refuge of being. The mortals we now name the mortals—not because their earthly life ends, but rather because they are capable of death as death. The mortals are who they are as mortals by essencing in the refuge of being. They are the essencing relationship to being as being.

Metaphysics, on the contrary, represents the human as an animal, as a living being. Even when the *ratio* reigns over the *animalitas*, the human being remains defined by life and lived experience. From rational living beings, the mortals must first come to be.

When we say: mortals, then we already think, in case we are thinking, the other three along with them from the single fold of the four.

Earth and sky, divinities and mortals belong together, united from themselves, in the single fold of the unifying fourfold. Each of the four in its way mirrors the essence of the remaining others again. Each is thus reflected in its way back into what is its own within the single fold of the four. This mirroring is no presentation of an image. Lighting up each of the four, this mirroring appropriates the essence of each to the others in a simple bringing into ownership [*einfältige Vereignung*]. In this appropriating-lighting way, each of the four reflectively plays with each of the remaining others. The appropriative mirroring releases each of the four into what is its own, while binding the ones so released to the single fold [*Einfalt*] of their essential reciprocality.

The mirroring that binds them to this space of freedom is the play that entrusts each of the four to the others by the folded support of this bringing into ownership. None of the four insists on its separate particularity. Each of the four within this bringing into ownership is much more expropriated to what is its own. This expropriative bringing into ownership is the mirror-play of the fourfold. From it is entrusted the single fold of the four.

We name the appropriating mirror-play of the single fold of the earth and sky, divinities and mortals, the world. The world essences in that it worlds. This says: The worlding of world is neither explicable by nor grounded upon anything other than itself. This impossibility is not a matter of our human thinking being incapable of such explaining and grounding. The inexplicability and ungroundability of the worlding of the world lies much more in the fact that things like causes and grounds remain unsuitable for the worlding of the world. As soon as human knowing reaches an explanation here, it does not somehow step over the essence of the world, but rather collapses beneath the essence of world. The human will to explain does not at all reach into what is simplistic of the single fold of worlding. The united four are already suffocated in their essence when one represents them only as individuated actualities that are grounded through one another and are to be explained in terms of each other.

The unity of the fourfold is the fouring. Indeed the fouring does not happen in such a way that it encloses the four and as this enclosure only comes to them belatedly. Just as little is the fouring limited to the four, once again present at hand, merely standing next to each other.

The fouring essences as the appropriating mirror-play of the ones that are simply entrusted to each other. The fouring essences as the worlding of world. The mirror-play of world is the round dance of appropriation [*Reigen des Ereignens*]. For this reason the round dance does not hug the four like a hoop. The round dance is a ring that rings by its play as a mirroring. Appropriating, it lights up the four in the gleam of their single fold. Gleaming, the ring everywhere openly brings the four into the ownership of the riddle of their essence. The collected essence of the mirror-play of the world, ringing in this way, is a circling [*das Gering*]. In the circling of this playfully-mirroring ring, the four nestle into their united essence and nonetheless each respectively into its own essence. Supple in this way, they join pliantly and worldingly the world.

Supple, lithesome, malleable, pliant, light, this is called in our old German language *ring* and *gering*. As what is slight about the ring [*das Gering des Ringes*], the mirror-play of the worlding world ringingly releases [*entringt*] the united four into their own pliancy, the nimbleness of their essence [*das Ringe ihres Wesens*]. From out of the mirror-play of the circling of the nimble [*des Gerings des Ringen*] there takes place the thinging of the thing.

The thing lets the fourfold abide. The thing things the world. Every thing lets the fourfold abide in something that each time abides from the single fold of the world.

When we let the thing in its thinging essence from out of the worlding world, then we commemorate the thing as thing. Thoughtfully remembering in this way, we allow the worlding essence of the thing to concernfully approach us. Thinking in this way we are met by the thing as thing. We are, in the strict sense of the word, conditioned [*Be-Dingten*]. We have left the arrogance of everything unconditional behind us.   ?

When we think the thing as thing, then we protect the essence of the thing in the region from where it essences. Thinging is the nearing of world. Nearing is the essence of nearness. Insofar as we protect the thing as thing, we dwell in nearness. The nearing of nearness is the authentic and sole dimension of the mirror-play of the world.

The exclusion of nearness despite all abolition of distances has brought the distanceless to dominance. In the exclusion of nearness, the thing as thing in the stated sense remains annihilated. But when and how are things as things? Thus we inquire amidst the dominance of the distanceless.

When and how do the things come as things? They do not come through the machinations of humans. But they also do not come without the vigilance of the mortals. The first step to such vigilance is the step back from merely representational, i.e., explanatory thinking into commemorative thinking.

The step back from one thinking into the other is admittedly no mere change of attitude. Indeed, it can never be something like that because all attitudes, along with the manner of their changing, remain stuck in the region of representational thinking. The step back, on the contrary, departs altogether from the domain of merely personal attitudes. Addressed by the world's essence from within it, the step back takes up its residence in a correspondence that answers this. For the arrival of the thing as thing, a mere change of attitude does nothing, just as all of what now stands in the distanceless as objects are never able on their own to transform themselves into things. The thing as thing also never comes about in our simply avoiding objects and remembering former old objects that perhaps were at one time on the way to becoming things or even to presencing as such.

Whatever becomes a thing, it takes place from out of the circling of the mirror-play of the world. Only when, presumably suddenly, the world worlds as world does the ring shine forth that ringingly releases the circling of earth and sky, divinities and mortals, into the nimbleness of its single fold [*das Ringe seiner Einfalt*].

In accordance with this circling, the thinging itself is slight and the thing that each time abides is nimble, inconspicuously pliant in its essence. The thing is nimble: jug and bench, footbridge and plow. But a thing is also, after its manner, tree and pond, stream and mountain. Things are, each abiding [*je weilig*] thing-like in its way, heron and deer, horse and bull. Things are, each abiding thing-like after their manner, mirror and clasp, book and picture, crown and cross.

Yet scant [*ring*] and slight [*gering*] are things even in number, as measured against the innumerable objects everywhere of equal value, as measured against the immeasurable masses of humans as living beings.

Humans as the mortals are the first to dwell in the world as world. Only what is slight of world ever becomes a thing.

Appendix

On the Thing lecture (for summary)

Thing and world referred to differentiation [*Unter-Schied*]. Cf. the Reisner letter.[7]

From this differentiation back to difference [*die Differenz*]. From this to the *forgetting* of beyng. How to think this? (Ἀ-λήθεια). A *forgetting* also remains—only transformed *after* the turn; does there then take place even the authentic harboring and sheltering from out of the counsel [*dem Ratsal*] itself?

From thing here to *world; world / wer-alt* <Old High German>.[8] Reference to the *difference*. Not a word with another meaning, but another *issue*.

The thinking that retrieves [Nach-*holendes Denken*] is commemorative thinking [*Andenken*]; to retrieve [*nach-holen*]—*to take into nearness* [in die Nähe holen].

The Differentiation [*Unter-schied*]

From this as the *jointure of beyng*—all joining of the saying— all rigor of the joining.

Thing

How everything presences.—presence—εἶναι. How "is" each thing? How does it stand with this "it is"?

Do the things thing? Are things as things?—or are they only as objects? And the objects—how do they stand? What is the manner of their stance and their constancy?—*as standing*

---

7. Letter to Prof. Dr. Reisner of November 3, 1950 <unpublished>.

8. Translator's Note: The Grimms' *Wörterbuch* provides this derivation of *Welt* (world) from *wer-alt*, though finds it a "difficult" one. *Wer* means "man" (as still heard in our word "werewolf") and *alt* comes from *alan*, meaning "generation, nurturance, growth." World (*Welt*) is thus the place wherein the human grows (and becomes old, *alt*). The derivation is said to parallel the Gothic translation of the Greek κόσμος by *manaseps*, "man seed," with the sense of world as a "life-supporting circle of human society" in contrast to the mortally dangerous wilderness. See *Deutsches Wörterbuch*, s.v. "Welt."

reserve? The things are gone, gone away—where to? In their place what has been—placed?

The things are as though long gone and nevertheless they have never yet been *as things.*

As things—never yet has their thing essence properly reached the light and been preserved.

What is horrifying announces and conceals itself in the way that the nearness nearby remains outstanding. What does this mean? It means: *the thing does not thing; the thing does not presence as thing.*

World does not world. Thing / World do not take place; the event of appropriation refuses itself. The differentiation remains forgotten; forgetting essences!

Thinging is not lit up as the essence of things and preserved as lit up. Even what lies far off presences—only for us, perhaps, because Dasein. But not the way to it; [nevertheless] this is something like it itself in its veiled <?> presencing.

The nearby can indeed be called in an emphatic sense that which presences.

In what lies nearby, nearness remains outstanding. In what presences, *presencing* withdraws. Because it withdraws itself and has so withdrawn, we never encounter it—least of all in the way that we are accustomed to encounter something—*in representation.*

Lying nearby are what we name things. What is this—a thing?

Positionality

The beginning of the path showed: all mastery of distances brings no nearness at all. With nearness there likewise slips away the remote. Everything is leveled down into the distanceless. Now we see more poignantly: Nearness essences insofar as the thing things. The thing things the world. Thinging is the nearing that holds the world as world in nearness. In nearing lies the essence of nearness.

Nearness is not shortness of distance, farness is not the length of distance. The remote is not at all the cancellation of nearness. Only with the nearing of nearness does the remote take its distance and remain guarded as the remote. For this reason, where the thing does not thing and nearness does not near, the remote, too, stays away. Nearness and farness remain equally outstanding. The distanceless dominates.

What one calls distance [*Abstand*] we know as the interval between two points. If we step outside the house under the tree and in its shadow, however, then admittedly the distance between house and tree does not rest in the measurement of the interval between them. The distance consists rather in that the house, tree, and shadow concernfully approach us from their mutual reciprocity, and also in how they do so. Such concerned approach attunes the distance (longinquity) between what is present within presencing. The distance to us of all that presences and absences is attuned by this concerned approach. Whatever has such distance, among themselves and to us, concernfully approaches us precisely by this distancing, be it that something lies far from us, be it that something comes near to us. Yet even what does not concern us, as

23

we say, in its own way does very much concernfully approach us. For the indifferent comes to concern us in that we constantly go past it and leave it alone.

Everything that presences and absences bears the character of what concernfully approaches. Distance lies in concerned approach. The concerned approach lies in nearness. We are too easily of the opinion that distance would consist in a standing opposite from us. On this account, distance appears to be first achieved in an opposition and first secured in the oppositional object. But the oppositional object is only the last term and the final remnant of what stands at a distance. When what presences becomes the oppositional object of a representation, the dominance of the distanceless has already installed itself, even if still unobtrusively. In the objective, what concernfully approaches us has been placed before us. Thus it stands away from us and we from it. Indeed, this objective representation, which by all appearances first lets us encounter what presences, is in its essence already an assault upon what concernfully approaches us. In the appearance of the purely present as proffered by the oppositional object, in the objective [*das Objektive*], there lies concealed the greed of representational calculation. Among what is oppositionally objective, there likewise belong the conditions in which we stand to ourselves, within which we monitor and dissect ourselves. Psychology and the dominance of psychological explanations contain the beginnings of the leveling down of the mental-spiritual into something that is accessible to everyone at all times and thus, at base, already distanceless. The dominance of what is oppositionally objective does not secure distance. Rather, there already lurks in it the insistence of the distanceless. If distance lies in concerned approach, then where the distanceless reigns we are really no longer approached concernfully by anything at all. Everything slides into the basic trait of the indifferent, even if here and there, like lost scatterings, much might still matter to us. The concernful approach of the indifferent is a wresting away into monotony that stops and starts, stands and falls, neither nearby nor far off. The distanceless [*Das Abstandlose*] so decisively concerns the human that he is approached in equal measure everywhere by what is uniformly without distance [*Distanzlosen*]. The equal measure of this approach by the distanceless consists in the fact that the human so approached continues ever anew to fall for the distanceless in the same empty ways. Whatever presences without distance [*ohne Abstand*] is nevertheless neither without concerned approach nor without a standing. Much to the contrary, the distanceless has its own standing. Its constancy makes the rounds in the uncanny concernful approach of what is everywhere of equal value. The human stands for this in lapsing into it. The distanceless is never without standing. It stands insofar as everything that presences is standing reserve. Where the standing reserve comes into power, even the object crumbles as characteristic of what presences.

The standing reserve persists. It persists insofar as it is imposed upon for a requisitioning. Directed into requisitioning, it is placed into application. Application positions everything in advance in such a manner that what is positioned follows upon a result. So placed, everything is: in consequence of. . . . The consequence, however, is ordered in advance as a success. A success is that type of consequence that itself remains assigned to the yielding of further consequences. The standing reserve persists through a characteristic positioning. We name it requisitioning [*das Be-Stellen*, to beset with positioning].

What does "to position, place, set" [*stellen*] mean? We know the word from the usages: to represent something [*etwas vor-stellen*, to place before], to produce something [*etwas her-stellen*, to place here]. Nevertheless we have to doubt whether our thinking is a match for even the simple and scarcely appreciated scope of these usages.

What does "to place, position, set" mean? Let us first consider it from production. The carpenter produces a table, but also a coffin. What is produced, set here, is not tantamount to the merely finished. What is set here stands in the purview of what concernfully approaches us. It is set here in a nearness. The carpenter in the village does not complete a box for a corpse. The coffin is from the outset placed in a privileged spot of the farmhouse where the dead peasant still lingers. There, a coffin is still called a "death-tree" [*Totenbaum*]. The death of the deceased flourishes in it. This flourishing determines the house and farmstead, the ones who dwell there, their kin, and the neighborhood.

Everything is otherwise in the motorized burial industry of the big city. Here no death-trees are produced.

A peasant positions his ox to drag fallen tree trunks out of the forest onto the path. He does not place the ox here just so that it would stand somewhere. He positions what is placed here in such a manner that it is directed toward application.

Men and women must place themselves in a work service. They are ordered. They are met by a positioning that places them, i.e., commandeers them. One places the other. He retains him. He positions him. He requires information and an accounting from him. He challenges him forth. Let us now enter into the meaning of this word "to position, place, set" so as to experience what comes to pass in that requisitioning through which an inventory arises [*der Bestand steht*] and is thus a standing reserve.

To place, position, set means here: to challenge forth, to demand, to compel toward self-positioning. This positioning occurs as a conscription [*die Gestellung*]. The demand for conscription is directed at the human. But within the whole of what presences, the human is not the only presence approached by conscription.

A tract of land is imposed upon, namely for the coal and ore that subsists in it. The subsistence of stone is presumably already conceived within the horizon of such a positioning and even only conceivable in terms of this. The subsisting stone that, as such, is already evaluated for a self-positioning is challenged forth and subsequently expedited along. The earth's soil is drawn into such a placing and is attacked by it. It is ordered, forced into conscription. This is how we understand the word "ordering" [*bestellen*] here and in what follows.

Through such requisitioning [*Bestellen*] the land becomes a coal reserve, the soil an ore depository.[1] This requisitioning is already of a different sort from that whereby the peasant had previously tended his field. Peasant activity does not challenge the farmland; rather it leaves the crops to the discretion of the growing forces; it protects them in their thriving. In the meantime, however, even the tending of the fields [*die Feldbestellung*] has gone over to the same requisitioning [*Be-Stellen*] that imposes upon the air for nitrogen, the soil for coal and ore, the ore for uranium, the uranium for atomic energy, and the latter

---

1. The soil, land—homelessness of the standing reserve!

for orderable destruction. Agriculture is now a mechanized food industry, in essence the same as the production of corpses in the gas chambers and extermination camps, the same as the blockading and starving of countries, the same as the production of hydrogen bombs.

But now what is it positioned toward, the coal that is positioned in the coal reserve, for example? It is not poised upon the table like the jug. The coal, for its part, is imposed upon, i.e., challenged forth, for heat, just as the ground was for coal; this heat is already imposed upon to set in place steam, the pressure of which drives the turbines, which keep a factory industrious, which is itself imposed upon to set in place machines that produce tools through which once again machines are set to work and maintained.

One positioning challenges the other, falls upon it with a conscripting. This does not proceed by a mere sequence of acts of positioning. According to its essence, conscription occurs in secret and in advance. Only for this reason does conscription make possible the planning and taking of action upon the individual motives of the particular positionings in a useful manner. But now where does this chain of requisitioning finally run off to?

The hydroelectric plant is placed in the river. It imposes upon it for water pressure, which sets the turbines turning, the turning of which drives the machines, the gearing of which imposes upon the electrical current through which the long-distance power centers and their electrical grid are positioned for the conducting of electricity.[2] The power station in the Rhine river, the dam, the turbines, the generators, the switchboards, the electrical grid—all this and more is there only insofar as it stands in place and at the ready, not in order to presence,[3] but to be positioned, and indeed solely to impose upon others thereafter.

Only what is so ordered that it stands in place and at the ready persists as standing reserve and, in the sense of standing reserve, is constant.[4] The constant consists of continuous orderability within such a conscription.

---

2. Standing reserve

3. in which way?

4. the word meant in the sense of an orderable standing reserve, i.e., not of a steady lasting [*stetig andauern*].

Again we ask: where does the chain of such requisitioning finally run out to? It runs out to nothing; for requisitioning produces nothing that could have, or would be allowed to have, a presence for itself outside of such positioning. What is ordered is always already and always only imposed upon to place another in the succession as its consequence. The chain of requisitioning does not run out to anything; rather it only enters into its circuit. Only in this does the orderable have its persistency [*Bestand*]. The Rhine river, for example, is there only as something ordered in the requisitioning just mentioned. The hydroelectric plant is not built in the Rhine river, but rather the river is built into the power plant and is what it is there due to the power plant's essence. In order to somewhat gauge the monstrosity that reigns here, let us attend only for a moment to the opposition expressed in the two names: The Rhine, built into the power plant—"The Rhine," as said in the artwork of Hölderlin's eponymous hymn.

The standing reserve persists [*Der Bestand besteht*]. It persists in requisitioning [*Bestellen*]. What is requisitioning in itself? Positioning [*das Stellen*] has the character of challenging forth. Accordingly it becomes an expediting along. This happens with the coal, the ore, the crude oil, with the rivers and seas, with the air. One says the earth is exploited in regard to the materials and forces hidden in it. This exploitation however is supposed to be the doing of humans and their ambition.

Accordingly, requisitioning would be a machination of the human, executed in the manner of an exploitation. The requisitioning of the standing reserve appears with this character, however, only as long as we represent it in the horizon of everyday opinion. This appearance, that requisitioning would be in its essence only a human machination with the character of exploitation, is even an unavoidable one. Nevertheless[5] it remains a mere illusion.

Requisitioning positions. It challenges forth. Requisitioning, however, when we consider it in its essence and not according to its possible effects, by no means goes toward spoils and profit, but rather always to the orderable. Here "always" means: from the outset, because essentially; the only reason requisitioning is

---

5. with technology as τέχνη—ἀ-λήθεια (Ἀ-λήθεια)

drawn from one orderable entity to the next is because, from the outset, requisitioning has wrested away all that presences and placed it into complete orderability, whether what presences in the particular case is especially positioned or not. This violence of requisitioning, outstripping everything, drags the particular acts of requisitioning only further along behind itself. This violence of requisitioning leads to the suspicion that what is here named "requisitioning" is no mere *human* doing, even if the human belongs to the carrying out of such a requisitioning.

The question remains in what way is the human already drawn into the essence of requisitioning. What (however) does this mean here: "the human"? "The human" exists nowhere. Assuming, though, that humans challenge forth the water power of the river for its pressure capacity and impose upon this to produce an electrical current, then humans are only capable of this insofar as they themselves are already ordered into this requisitioning. Humans, in their relation to what presences, are already challenged in advance, and therefore everywhere, and thus constantly, to represent what presences as something orderable for a requisitioning. Insofar as human representation has already posited what presences as something orderable in the calculation of a requisitioning, the human remains, according to his essence and whether knowingly or not, ordered into a requisitioning for the requisitioning of the orderable.

The human himself stands now[6] within such a conscription. The human has offered himself for the carrying out of this conscripting. He stands in line to take over such requisitioning and to complete it. The human is thereby an employee of requisitioning. Humans are thus, individually and in masses, assigned into this. The human is now the one ordered in, by, and for the requisitioning.

Requisitioning is no human deed; in order for human effectiveness to cooperate each time in the requisitioning, as it does, it must already be orderable by this requisitioning for a corresponding doing and allowing.

Requisitioning not only assaults the materials and forces of nature with a conscripting. Requisitioning assaults at the same time the destiny of the human. The essence of the human is

---

6. vague—now thought essentially in the manner of positionality

imposed upon to collaborate in carrying out the requisitioning in a human manner. Requisitioning comes upon nature and history, all that is, and in every way that whatever presences is. What presences is imposed upon as such for orderability and thus represented in advance as something[7] steady, whose standing essences from requisitioning. What is constant in such a way and constantly present is the standing reserve.

Consequently, requisitioning can never be explained by any single item of standing reserve, just as little as it can be conceived from the sum of items of standing reserve at hand as a universal that would just hover above them. Requisitioning cannot be explained at all, i.e., it cannot be led back to something clear. We unwittingly pass off as clear everything that is readily and commonly known to us and generally held to be unquestionable. What we are in the habit of explaining by something clear is always merely rendered unconsidered and thoughtless. We are not able to explain the requisitioning wherein the standing reserve essences.[8] Rather, we must first of all attempt to experience its still unthought essence.

For this it is necessary that we observe how requisitioning from the outset attacks everything that is: Nature and history, humans, and divinities; for if an ill-advised theology today orders the results of modern atomic physics so as to secure with their help its proofs for the existence of God, then in so doing God is placed into the realm of the orderable.

Requisitioning affects all that presences in respect to its presence[9] with a conscripting. Requisitioning is only directed at one thing, *versus unum,* namely to position *the one whole* of what presences as standing reserve. Requisitioning is in itself universal. It gathers in itself all possible types of placing and all manner of their linking. In itself, requisitioning is already gathered for the continual securing of the status of the orderability of *all* that presences as standing reserve.

We name the collection of mountains [*der Berge*] that are already gathered together, united of themselves and never belatedly, the mountain range [*das Gebirge*]. We name the collection

---

7. so ordered and thus in this sense
8. to the extent that explanation leads away from the issue at stake
9. presencing—why, from where?

of ways we are inclined to such and such [*zumute ist*] and can feel ourselves so inclined, disposition [*das Gemüt*].

We now name the self-gathered collection of positioning [*des Stellens*], wherein everything orderable essences in the standing reserve, *positionality* [das Ge-Stell].

This word now no longer names an individual object of the sort like a bookcase or a water well.[10] Positionality now also does not name something constant in the ordered standing reserve. Positionality names the universal ordering, gathered of itself, of the complete orderability of what presences as a whole. The circuit of ordering takes place in positionality and as positionality.

In positionality the presencing of all that presences becomes standing reserve. Positionality constantly draws what is orderable into the circuit of requisitioning, establishes it therein, and thus assigns it as something constant in the standing reserve. The assignment does not place what is constant outside of the circuit of positioning. It only assigns it, but off and away into a subsequent orderability, i.e., back and forth into a requisitioning.

Positionality positions. It wrests everything together into orderability. It reaps everything that presences into orderability and is thus the gathering of this reaping [*Raffens*]. Positionality is a plundering [*Geraff*]. But this reaping never merely piles up inventory. Much more, it reaps away what is ordered into the circuit of orderability. Within the circuit, the one positions the other. The one drives the other ahead, but ahead and away into requisitioning.

The collected positioning of positionality is the gathering of self-circulating impulse [*Treibens*]. Positionality is drive [*Getriebe*]. The plundering reaps and indeed reaps away into the drive of industry.

Positionality essences as the plundering drive that orders the constant orderability of the complete standing reserve.

What we thereby think as *positionality* is the essence of technology.

---

10. still sharper contrast with composition [*Montage*], rod assemblies and pistons [*Gestänge und Geschiebe*]; skeletal structure [*Gerippe*]

We say "technology" and mean modern technology. One likes to characterize it as machine technology. This characterization hits upon something correct. But what is correct about it still contains no truth, for it does not reveal anything of the essence of modern technology, and indeed it does not do so because the manner of representing that this characterization of modern technology as machine technology stems from is never able to reveal the essence of technology. One is of the opinion that modern technology, as distinct from all previous forms, would be defined by the machine. But what if it were the reverse? Modern technology is what it is not through the machine, but rather the machine is only what it is and how it is from the essence of technology. Thus one says nothing of the essence of modern technology when one conceives it as machine technology.

From the outset, positionality as such imposes upon all standing reserve that it only persist through the machine. To what extent? Positionality is the gathering of the drive's plundering of the constancy of the orderable, which itself is solely imposed upon such that it would stand in place and at the ready. Positionality is the collected requisitioning of the orderable that circulates in itself. Positionality is in itself the reaping, impulsive circulation of the requisitioning of the orderable in the ordering. Positionality imposes this equality of the orderable upon everything, that everything constantly position itself again in equivalent form and indeed in the equality of orderability.

Positionality, as this circulation in itself of requisitioning, composes the essence of the machine. Rotation belongs to this, though not necessarily in the form of a wheel, for the wheel is defined by rotation, not rotation by wheels. Rotation is that revolving which courses back into itself, driving on the orderable (propellant) into the requisitioning of the orderable (propulsion). The rotation of the machine is positioned, i.e., challenged forth, and made constant in the circulation that lies in drive, the essential character of positionality.

Long before the end of the eighteenth century, when the first machines were invented and set running in England, positionality, the essence of technology, was already afoot in a concealed manner. This says: the essence of technology already reigned beforehand, so much so that it first of all lit up the region within which the invention of something like power-producing machines could at all be sought out and attempted.[11]

Consequently, we may describe ever so expertly the most modern machine and explain its construction with great precision, nevertheless we grasp the machine always only technologically. We never think the machine from out of the *essence* of technology. Yet the essence of technology is itself nothing technological. Every construction of every machine already moves within the essential space of technology. As technological construction, however, it is never capable of conceptualizing the *essence* of the machine. This is just as impossible an attempt as wishing to calculate the essence of the mathematical by mathematical means, or wishing to delineate the essence of history through historiological research.

Along our way it must suffice to show the essential place of the machine. The machine is nothing that separately presences for itself. It is by no means merely a more developed sort of tool and apparatus, merely a self-propelled wheel assembly, as distinct from the spinning wheel of the peasant woman or the bucket wheel in the rice fields of China. The machine does not at all merely step into the place of equipment and tools. The machine is just as little an object. It stands only insofar as it goes. It goes insofar as it runs. It runs in the drive of industry. The drive drives as the bustle of the requisitioning of the orderable. If the machine stands, then its standstill is a condition of the drive, of its cessation or disturbance. Machines are within a machinery. But this is no piling up of machines. The machinery runs from the plundering of the drive, as which positionality orders the standing reserve.

Even when not immediately and not instantly perceived, positionality has already from the outset abolished all those places where the spinning wheel and water mill previously stood. Through its machinery, positionality orders in advance another kind of positioning and its regime. In this there only comes to stand that which stands in place, uniformly at the ready as orderable.

---

11. an essential consequence of this illuminated clearing is modern physics—which rests in *objectivity;*—the sphere itself as *discovery.*

Thus the manner by which the machine itself produces something is also essentially different from handicraft activity, assuming that there is still anything at all like craft production within positionality.

The tractors and automobiles are brought out, spewed out, serially piece by piece. But where out there does something put out in this manner stand? Into what standing is it so brought?

The automobile is put out in such a way that it is in place and at the ready, i.e., immediately and constantly deliverable. It is not produced so that it would stand there and remain standing there like the jug. The automobile is much more imposed upon to leave and indeed as something orderable that, for its part, can be challenged forth precisely for a further conducting along, which itself sets in place the promotion of commerce.

What the machines put out piece-by-piece they put into the standing reserve of the orderable. That which is put out is a piece of the standing reserve [*Bestand-Stück*]. This word is now used in a strict and new sense.

The piece [*das Stück*] is something other than the part [*der Teil*]. The part shares itself with parts in a whole. It takes part in the whole, belongs to it.[12] The piece on the contrary is separated and indeed, as the piece, is even isolated from the other pieces. It never shares itself with these in a whole. The piece of standing reserve does not even share itself with its own kind in the standing reserve. The standing reserve is much more that which has been shattered [*Zerstückte*] into the orderable. This shattering does not break apart, but instead precisely creates the standing reserve of the pieces of inventory. Each of these is loaded into and confined in a circuit of orderability. The isolating of piece from piece corresponds to the confining of everything that has been isolated in an industry of requisitioning.[13]

If one wanted to take away, piece by piece and all together, the pieces of inventory in a fleet [*Bestand*] of automobiles and put them somewhere else, then the pieces would be torn out of the circuit of their orderability. The result would be some kind of automobile graveyard. The parking lot is something different, since there every car in its orderability stands at the

---

12. completes its wholeness
13. unity of the standing reserve—how?

ready and is the positioned piece of an ordered standing reserve of ordering.

The pieces of the standing reserve are piece-for-piece equivalent. Their character as pieces demands this uniformity. As equivalent the pieces are isolated against one another in the extreme; just in this way they heighten and secure their character as pieces. The uniformity of the pieces provides that one piece can be exchanged for the other without further ado, i.e., is in place for this, and thus stands at the ready. One piece of standing reserve is replaceable by another. The piece as piece is already imposed upon for replaceability. Piece of standing reserve means: that which is isolated, as a piece, is interchangeably confined within a requisitioning.

Even that which we name a machine part is, strictly thought, never a part. Indeed it fits into the gearing, but as an exchangeable piece. My hand, on the contrary, is not a piece of me. I myself am entirely in each gesture of the hand, every single time.

With the name "piece" we commonly represent to ourselves something lifeless, although one also speaks of a piece of livestock. The pieces of the standing reserve are nevertheless each time loaded into a requisitioning and positioned by this. Admittedly, the human also belongs to what has been so positioned, though in his own way, be it that he serves the machine, be it that he constructs and builds the machine within the requisitioning of the machinery.[14] In the age of technological dominance, the human is placed into the essence of technology, into positionality, by his essence. In his own way, the human is a piece of the standing reserve in the strictest sense of the words "piece" and "standing reserve."

The human is exchangeable within the requisitioning of the standing reserve. That he is a piece of the standing reserve remains the presupposition for the fact that he can become the functionary of a requisitioning. Yet the human belongs in positionality in a wholly other way than the machine does. This way can become inhuman. The *in*human, however, is ever still in*human*. The human never becomes a machine. The inhuman and yet human is admittedly more uncanny, while more evil and ominous, than the human who would merely be a machine.

---

14. this way exceptional—despite all the uniformity

The human of this age, however, is positioned into position-ality even when he does not stand immediately before ma-chines or in the industry of a machinery. The forester, for ex-ample, who surveys the felled wood in the forest and who to all appearances still goes along the same paths in the same way as his grandfather is today positioned by the lumber industry. Whether he knows it or not, he is in his own way a piece of inventory in the cellulose stock and its orderability for the paper that is delivered to the newspapers and tabloids that impose themselves upon the public sphere so as to be devoured by it.

Radio and film belong to the standing reserve of this requi-sitioning through which the public sphere as such is positioned, challenged forth, and thereby first installed. Their machineries are pieces of inventory in the standing reserve, which bring everything into the public sphere and thus order the public sphere for anyone and everyone without distinction. For the installation and guidance of the public sphere, the pieces of in-ventory of this standing reserve are not only the machinery, but, in their way, the employees of this industry as well, up to the public broadcast advisory council. This is positioned by the standing reserve called the radio, i.e., challenged forth to the ordering of this industry. As a piece of inventory of this stand-ing reserve, the council remains confined in it. Let us just for once posit the unlikely case that a public broadcast advisory council recommended the abolition of the radio. The council would be dismissed overnight and indeed because it only is what it is as something positioned of a standing reserve in the positionality of the ordering of the public sphere.

Every radio listener who turns its dial is isolated in the piece character of the pieces of the standing reserve, isolated as a piece of the standing reserve, in which he remains con-fined even if he still thinks he is entirely free to turn the de-vice on and off. Indeed, he is only still free in the sense that each time he must free himself from the coercive insistence of the public sphere that nevertheless ineluctably persists.

Humans are not incidentally pieces of the standing reserve of the radio. They are in their essence already imposed upon with the character of having to be a piece of standing reserve. Let us again suppose, indeed, a more unlikely case, that sud-denly everywhere across the earth the radio receivers were to disappear from every room—who would be able to fathom the cluelessness, the boredom, the emptiness that would attack the human at a stroke and would completely dishevel their everyday affairs?

Note that here there is no passing of judgment on the radio listener or even on radio. It is only a matter of pointing out that in the standing reserve called the radio there reigns a requisitioning and positioning that has intervened in the essence of the human. Because this is so, and because the human does not decide about his essence on his own terms, and never by himself, for this reason the requisitioning of the standing reserve, for this reason positionality, the essence of technology, cannot be anything merely human. For this reason one ultimately errs in attempting to derive technology from human intelligence, even from artistic intelligence. The artistic presupposes the *ars*, the *ars* presupposes τέχνη, and this presupposes the essence of technology.

The standing reserve of positionality persists in the pieces of standing reserve and in the manner of their ordering. The pieces of standing reserve are what is constant in the standing reserve. For this reason, we must think their constancy from the essence of the standing reserve, i.e., from positionality.

One commonly conceives the constant as that which endures. This is something that presences lastingly. But what presences can concernfully approach the human in varying ways of presence. These varying ways determine the epochs of the Western history of beyng. What presences can essence as what here comes forth of its own accord, here from out of concealment, forth into unconcealment. We name what presences in this way in its presencing "that which stands here" [*Herstand*].

What presences can announce itself as something created by a maker, who himself is a constant and omnipresent presence in everything. What presences can offer itself as what is posed in human representation, for it and across from it. What presences is thus an oppositional object for representation; representation, as *percipere*, is the *cogitare* of the *ego cogito*, of the *conscientia*, of consciousness, of the self-consciousness of the subject. What stands over against [*der Gegenstand*] is the object [*das Objekt*] for the subject.

What is present, however, can also be something constant in the sense of the pieces of inventory of the standing reserve, which, as the constantly orderable, are placed into that positioning as which positionality reigns.

Positionality is the essence of technology. Its positioning is universal. It addresses itself to the unity of the whole of all that presences. Positionality thus sets in place the way that everything present now presences. All that is, in the most manifold of ways and variations and whether obviously or in a still hidden manner, is a piece of inventory of the standing reserve in the requisitioning of positionality. The constant consists in an orderable replaceability by an ordered equivalent.

The essence of technology is positionality. Positionality orders. It orders what is present through conscription. Positionality orders what is present into standing reserve. What is constant of the standing reserve are the pieces of standing reserve. Their constancy consists in the orderable replaceability of the steadily equivalent, which is in place and at the ready. But here a consideration arises. If the essence of technology consists in positionality, but technology seeks to impose upon the forces and materials of nature, i.e., seeks to challenge them forth as that which, expedited along, conducts everything toward a successful result, then precisely the essence of technology itself reveals that it is not universal. The forces and materials of nature set so decisive a limit for technology that technology remains referred to nature as the source and backing of its technological standing reserve. For this reason, we would not be able to proclaim that everything that presences would essence in the manner of something constant, something that comes to a stand in the requisitioning of positionality. Positionality does not concern all that presences. Technology is only one actuality among other actualities. To be sure, technology remains far from constituting the actuality of everything actual.

What is the status of the essence of technology? Is it universal or not? What is the relationship between technology and nature?

Indeed what is this nature that is supposed to presence outside the realm of the technological standing reserve as that to which the requisitioning must ever again return? How does nature presence, insofar as technology, which is dependent upon nature, takes from it the forces of its power plants as well as their materials? What are the forces of nature that are positioned in technology? The answer is provided by the natural sciences. The fundamental discipline of the science of the physical is physics. This tells us nothing, to be sure, about the essence of force. But physics provides thinking with an opportunity to pursue how the natural sciences conceive what they name "force." Physically, natural force is only accessible in its effects, for only in its effects does force demonstrate the calculability of a magnitude. In this calculation, force becomes objective. Only as this object of calculation does it concern natural science. Nature is represented as something actual, placed into measure and number, and presencing objectively in its having acted. This having acted, once again, only counts as presencing insofar as it itself takes effect and proves itself as effective. That which presences of nature is the actual. The actual is the effectual. The presencing of nature consists in effectiveness. In this, nature can bring something into place and set it at the ready, i.e., let it succeed.

Force is that which imposes upon something so that something else follows from it in an assessable manner. The natural forces are represented by physics in the sense of a positioning by means of which positionality places what presences. Nature stands over and against technology in this way and this way only, in that nature as a system for the requisitioning of consequences consists of something effectual and positioned. Kant thought this essence of nature for the first time and set the standard, though without going back to positionality. The effectiveness of the actual—nature—is nothing other than the capacity for the ordering of consequences. This says: nature stands over against technology not as something indeterminately presencing on its own. It does not at all stand over against technology as an object that is opportunely exploited. In the world era of technology, nature belongs in advance in the standing reserve of the orderable within positionality.[15]

One will object, this may be so, to the detriment of those forces of nature that are, so to speak, tapped by technology. But natural materials, on the contrary, since long ago, long before technology began, lie outside of the technological standing reserve. Chemistry establishes what the materials are in themselves, in their objective actuality.

---

15. atomic physics

But how does science take the material of nature? It conceives it as matter. What is the fundamental characteristic of matter for physics? It is inertia. What does the physicist understand by inertia? Physically conceived, inertia is continuance in a state of motion. Rest is also such a state, which counts in a physically calculable manner as the limit case of motion. Inertia is resistance against the change of motion. Resistance is a countereffect and indeed against acceleration. As matter, the material is represented in the horizon of motion and in regard to the effectual, i.e., represented in terms of the force that is expended, i.e., must be in place, in order to change the respective state of motion, i.e., to order another one.

For physics, nature is the standing reserve of energy and matter. They are the pieces of the standing reserve of nature. With respect to inertia, matter is determined by energy. Energy, however, is the effectual, the ordering capacity for the ordered positioning of a consequence. Force itself is something orderable that is capable of ordering; it is orderable for its conservation, transformation, and storage capacities—such a cast of characters assigned to a constantly positionable orderability of energy.

Not only natural forces, but also the natural materials are physically-chemically represented as ordering-orderable standing reserve; represented in an essential ambiguity of this word "represented" [*vor-gestellt*], namely, positioned beforehand and then with regard to the calculation of outcomes.

Due to the essence of technology, nature, which to all appearances stands over and against technology, is already inserted into the standing reserve of positionality as the fundamental standing reserve. Historically, the essence of modern technology begins its reign with the commencement of modern natural science some three and a half centuries ago. What does this say? It does not say that modern technology initially would have been merely natural science and then only later would have emerged as the application of this. It says instead: the essence of modern technology, positionality, in accordance with its essence, began with the fundamental act of requisitioning insofar as it first secured nature in advance as the fundamental standing reserve. Modern technology is not applied natural science, far more is modern natural science the application of the essence of technology, wherein the latter directs itself to its fundamental standing reserve so as to secure it in applicability.

For natural science, something only counts as presencing when it is calculable in advance and only insofar as it is. The predictability of natural processes, standard for all natural scientific representing, is the representational orderability of nature as the standing reserve of a succession. Whether this calculability turns out to be univocal and certain or merely remains probable and only conceivable statistically does not alter in the least the essence of nature as standing reserve, the only essence of nature admitted by the essence of technology.[16] To be sure, atomic physics is experimentally and calculably of a different sort than classical physics. Thought in terms of its essence, however, it nevertheless remains the same physics.

In the world age of technology, nature is no limit of technology. There, nature is much more the fundamental piece of inventory of the technological standing reserve—and nothing else.

Nature is no longer even an object [Gegen-stand]. As the fundamental piece of the standing reserve in positionality, it is something constant whose standing and steadiness is determined solely by requisitioning. All that presences, even nature, essences in the manner of something constant in the standing reserve that positionality orders.

In its positioning, positionality is universal. It concerns all that presences; everything, not only in sum and sequentially, but everything insofar as everything that presences as such is here positioned in its very consistency by a requisitioning. Thus it changes nothing whether we properly note and establish this character of presencing every time and immediately, or, what is much more the case, whether we overlook it for a long time and continue to conceive the actuality of the actual in a customary manner, one that, strictly thought, is thoroughly confused.[17]

---

16. the machines—the atomic processes and the corresponding methods

17. cf. "Science and Reflection." Translator's Note: a 1953 lecture first published in *Vorträge und Aufsätze* in 1954, see Martin Heidegger, *Vorträge und Aufsätze, Gesamtausgabe* vol. 7, ed. Friedrich-Wilhelm von Herrmann (Frankfurt a.M.: Vittorio Klosterman, 2000), 37–65. English translation: "Science and Reflection," in Martin Heidegger, *The Question Concerning Technology and Other Essays,* ed. and trans. William Lovitt (New York: Harper & Row, Publishers, 1977), 155–82.

In the world age of technology all that presences does so after the manner of the constancy of the pieces of inventory in the standing reserve. Even the human presences in this way, even if from time to time and in places he appears as though his essence and presence were not approached by the positioning of positionality.

The constancy of the piece of standing reserve is characterized by uniformity. In positionality, everything is imposed upon for the constant replaceability of the equivalent by the equivalent. Only in this way does positionality remain completely reaped into the constancy of its drive. Positionality reaps everything orderable in advance into the equivalence of the unrestricted orderability of the complete standing reserve. A constantly exchangeable equivalence holds equally in everything constant. The equivalence of value in everything constant secures for this its constancy through a replaceability that is orderable and in place. The standing reserve consists of the requisitioning of positionality. In the standing reserve everything stands in equal value. The standing reserve orders the distanceless.

Everything actual converges in the uniformly distanceless. The nearness and farness of what presences remain outstanding. Our meditation began from this point of reference. The airplane and all the apparatus of commerce continually increasing in speed serve to shorten distances. Everyone knows this today. Everything ensures that the earth becomes smaller. Everyone knows: this is effected by technology.

We possess this insight without needing to go down such roundabout paths as those we have now gone down, in that we considered the thing and its thinging, positionality and its positioning, the standing reserve and its pieces.

Why do we nevertheless follow this path of thinking in order to achieve insight into that which is? Because we by no means wish to ascertain only or even just for once an arbitrarily increasable number of observations that everyone is familiar with in the technological age. What is decisive is not that the distances are diminishing with the help of technology, but rather that nearness remains outstanding. We also do not merely ascertain this. We consider the essence of nearness and do so in order to experience to what extent it remains outstanding, in order to consider what takes place in this exclusion.[18] We do not pursue the aftereffects of technology in order to sketch its consequences. We think into the essence of technology in order to experience how, according to its essence, this excluding of nearness is implicated in the essential unfolding of technology. The machines of technology are only able to shorten distances, but nonetheless bring no nearness because the essence of technology from the outset does not allow nearness and farness. However, by no means do we consider the essence of technology in order to construct the edifice of a philosophy of technology or even merely to outline such a philosophy. Technology essences as positionality. But what reigns in positionality? From where and how does the essence of positionality take place?[19]

---

18. Why exactly nearness? Nearness and *differentiation!*
19. positionality as "essence" in the broad sense

The Danger

Positionality orders the standing reserve. Prior to this, positionality also prohibits nearness. Nearness remains outstanding in positionality, which everywhere arranges what is distanceless of the equally valued. This provides a hint into the essence of positionality, for it presumably belongs to the essence of positionality that the exclusion of nearness takes place in it because positionality essences in such a manner that it prohibits nearness.

What takes place when nearness is withheld? How does the essence of positionality thereby essence? Nearness nears. Nearness brings the world near.[1]

But world is the still-concealed mirror-play of the fourfold of heaven and earth, mortals and divinities. To bring the world near is the thinging of the thing. Should the nearness that brings near be prohibited, then the thing as thing remains withheld.

The universal requisitioning of positionality allows all that presences to presence solely as pieces of inventory of the standing reserve. In the standing reserve, objects are no longer permitted, much less the thing as thing. Positionality essences in that it does not yet guard the thing as thing. In the essence of positionality the thing remains unguarded as thing. Positionality's essence lets the thing go without guard. In our language, where it still inceptually speaks, the word "guard" [*die Wahr*] means protection. In our Swabian dialect this word "guard" means a child entrusted to maternal protection. Positionality in its positioning lets the thing go without protection—without the guard of its

---

1. Distance and nearness

essence as thing.[2] Positionality's essence does not guard the thing as thing. Positionality essences in that it leaves the thing unguarded. But because positionality reigns from long ago, though concealed, and through its requisitioning ever more decisively wrests away all that presences into standing reserve, under this essential domination of positionality the thing as thing has long become ever more unguarded. In the plundering of its drive, which everywhere secures solely the orderable standing reserve, positionality reaps the thing, inceptually unguarded in its essence, away into greater and greater neglect.

In the essence of positionality, the unguarding of the thing as thing takes place.

The word "unguarding" [*Verwahrlosung*] is here taken literally and this means: it is spoken from out of a previously thought issue; for what is genuinely thought is rightly said and the genuinely said is rightly thought. Unguarding here does not mean a slipping into neglect, does not signify a decay into disorder. The word "unguarding" as now used is no term of derision; it entails no value judgment at all. The unguarding of the thing names what proceeds from the essence of positionality, signaling to us the essence of technology.

What takes place in the unguarding of the thing? What has already occurred if the thing is not yet able to thing as a thing?

In thinging, the thing brings the world near and lets the world abide. If the thing, unguarded as it is, does not thing, then the world as world remains denied. In the unguarding of the thing there takes place the refusal of world.

But world is the still-concealed mirror-play of the fourfold of sky and earth, mortals and divinities.

The world worlds. But the worlding of world is not only not properly experienced and correspondingly thought, but even more we are still entirely inept at both thinking the worlding of the world purely on its own terms and at corresponding to this.[3] Thus we require assistance. Admittedly, instead of thinking the worlding of world on its own terms in a corresponding way of thinking, this assistance compels us to conceive that worlding

---

2. only this! does not the exclusion of the essence of truth take place in the dispensation?

3. The event of appropriation

by starting from something other than itself. This something else, starting from which we now representatively think the worlding of the world, again cannot be entirely foreign to the essence of world. Quite to the contrary, it occurs to us that we take this something else, from which we understand the worlding of the world, to be the essence of world, while in truth the worlding of the world is precisely the concealed essence of what we drag in here to characterize the worlding of world. Thus we proceed knowingly along an unavoidable, erroneous path. But because we go along it knowingly we can turn back at any time.

World is the fourfold of earth and sky, divinities and mortals. In the uniting whole of its presence, the mirror-play of the fouring guards everything that thingingly presences and absences between the four. From long ago the presence of what presences, of τὸ ἐόν, the being [*das Seiend*] is called τὸ εἶναι, being [*das Sein*], namely the being of the ἐόντα, of the being, the *esse entium*.

World lets the thinging of the thing take place, clearing-guarding it. World thus guards the essence of presencing as such. World guards worldingly the essence of that which essences as the being of beings.

We conceive the world now in terms of what is familiar to us, the being of beings. So conceived, the world is what guards being in its essence. Guarding in such a way, the world is the guardian of the essence of being. Instead of guardianship [*Wahrnis*] we also say truth [*Wahrheit*] and thereby think this basic word more inceptually from out of the worlding of world.

In the fourfold of earth and sky, divinities and mortals, the still-concealed mirror-play worlds as the world. The world is the truth of the essence of being.

Thus we now characterize the world in respect to being. So conceived, world is subordinate to being, while in truth the essence of being essences from out of the concealed worlding of world.[4] World is not one way of being and deferential to this. Being has to own its essence from the worlding of world. This points out that the worlding of world is an appropriating [*das Ereignen*] in a still-unexperienced sense of this word. When world first properly takes place, then being, and along with it the nothing, vanish into worlding. Only when the nothing, in

---

4. (Event of appropriation)

its essence from the truth of being, vanishes into this is nihilism overcome.

But world still refuses itself as world. World still withdraws into the concealment proper to it.

To remain concealed is called in Greek λανθάνειν. Λήθη is concealment. World, in its self-refusing worlding, remains concealed as the essential provenance of being. Yet world remains in concealment (Λήθη) in such a way that its concealment precisely affords an unconcealment:[5] the Ἀλήθεια. This is the lighting sheltering of the presencing of what presences in its unconcealment. The being in its being essences as something present from out of Ἀλήθεια. In the unconcealment of what presences as such, in Ἀλήθεια, there rests the full essential richness of the dispensation of the being of all beings, and from there it is dispensed.

Ἀλήθεια sends itself into the lighting sheltering of presencing; it proceeds to unfold what presences into what is dispensational of its presencing. Ἀλήθεια is the dispensation of being, as which dispensation the fullness of the history of being is joined in its epochs. Ἀ-λήθεια, the unconcealment of what presences as such, however, essences only when and only for as long as concealment, Λήθη, takes place. For Ἀλήθεια does not abolish Λήθη. Unconcealment does not consume concealment, but instead unconcealment constantly requires concealment and in this way confirms it as the essential source of Ἀλήθεια. The latter keeps to Λήθη and sustains itself in it. This, however, so decisively that even Ἀλήθεια itself as such,[6] early on, falls back into concealment in favor of what presences as such. What presences assumes priority over that wherein alone it essences. For presencing, i.e., enduring and continuing here in the clearing of a worldly openness, can only essence insofar as unconcealment takes place, whether this be experienced for itself and even conceived or not. In fact Ἀλήθεια does not properly guard itself in its own essence. It lapses into concealment, Λήθη. Ἀλήθεια falls into forgetfulness. In no way does this consist in merely not retaining a human representation in the memory somehow; rather forgetfulness, the lapsing into concealment, takes place with Ἀλήθεια itself in favor of the essence of what

5. disclosure
6. guards, remains back—and consequently first ὀρθότης

presences, which presences within unconcealment. Λήθη is the forgetfulness of the guardianship of the essence of being. So construed, Λήθη is precisely the essential source and essential provenance of the reign of every way of being. The abbreviated and therefore easy-to-misunderstand expression "forgetting of being" says that both the essence of being, presencing, and its essential provenance in Ἀλήθεια as the event of the essence of this, as well as Ἀλήθεια itself, all lapse into forgetfulness.[7] With this lapsing into concealment, the essence of Ἀλήθεια and of presencing withdraw. Insofar as they withdraw, they remain[8] inaccessible to human perception and representation. For this reason, human thinking is unable to think the essence of unconcealment or the presencing in it. So construed, unable to thoughtfully remember, human thinking from the outset has forgotten the essence of being. But human thinking is only in such a forgetfulness of the essence of being because this essence itself has taken place as forgetfulness, as a lapsing into concealment.[9] This event rests upon the world, as guardian of the essence of being, refusing itself. The hint that such refusal takes place conceals itself in the dispensation of being, a dispensation that joins in with the epochs of the forgetfulness of being so much so that these epochs, precisely as epochs of the disclosure of beings in their beinghood, are the epochs that determine Western-European history up to its contemporary unfolding as planetary totality. This is the presupposition for the fact that the modern battle for mastery of the earth is concentrated upon the positions of the two contemporary "world" powers.

Refusal of world takes place as the unguarding of the thing.[10] Refusal of world and unguarding of the thing are in a singular relationship. As this relationship, they are the same, although not equivalent.

In what way does the refusal of world take place as the unguarding of the thing? In the way that positionality essences. It orders all that is present as what is constant of the pieces of

---

7. remains in it

8. immediately

9. Forgetting of differentiation: unguarding of the thing—refusal of world

10. of presence

inventory of the standing reserve. In so ordering the standing reserve, positionality places all that is present into a state of distancelessness. Positionality concerns the presencing of all that presences as such. Positionality is thus in its essence the being of beings in its most extreme and presumably completed destiny.

Positionality is the essence of modern technology. The essence of positionality is the being of beings itself, not everywhere and not from time immemorial, but rather now, here where the forgetting of the essence of being completes itself. The event of this completion of the forgetting of being determines the epoch first of all, in that being now essences in the manner of positionality. It is the epoch of the completed unguarding of the thing by positionality. World, however, which worldingly appropriates the thinging of the thing, remains concealed, although it is precisely its concealment that affords the unconcealment of what presences, and thus of presencing, the being of beings. Preserving the truth of the essence of being and dispensing being in its destiny, the world is being itself.

Thoroughly dominating what presences as such in the manner of the unguarding of the thing, positionality is being itself.

World and positionality are the same. But once again: the same is never the equivalent. The same is just as little a merely undifferentiated confluence of the identical. The same is much more the relation of differentiation. In the taking place of this relation [Verhältnis], what is the same is necessarily held [gehalten] in it, i.e., is protected in it, i.e., is preserved in it, and thus in the strong sense of the word remains reserved [verhalten]. World and positionality are the same and thus, to the very extremes of their essence, set against one another.

But the contrariety of world and positionality is no mere present-at-hand antagonism, something representable between present-at-hand objects. The contrariety takes place. It takes place within the same as what essences of being itself. By ordering all that presences into the standing reserve, positionality sets the presencing of what presences outside of its essential provenance, outside of Ἀλήθεια. Ordering the standing reserve, positionality allows the dominance of the distanceless. Everything counts as equal. For what is of equal value, it is no longer a matter of whether and how it itself still presences as unconcealed against something else, something concealed.

Ordering the standing reserve, positionality allows uncon-cealment and its essence to lapse into full forgetting. Position-ality as the essence of being transposes being outside of the truth of its essence, ousts [*entsetzt*] being from its truth.

In the essencing of positionality, being itself is ousted from the truth of its essence, without however at any time in this displacement and self-unseating being able to sunder itself from the essence of beyng. Insofar as positionality essences, the guardianship of the essence of being, i.e. the world, sets itself under the dominance of a positionality that refuses the world through the unguarding of the thing.

Thus in the essence and reign of positionality, the arrival of the worlding of world is withheld. Yet precisely this event of the withholding of world maintains a hidden distance [*Ferne*] to the worlding of world.[11]

In positionality as the completed destiny of the forgetting of the essence of being, a ray from the distant arrival of world in-conspicuously shines. Insofar as world refuses its worlding, what happens with world is not nothing, but rather from refusal there radiates the lofty nearness of the most distant distance of world.

World and positionality are the same. They are differently the essence of being. World is the guardian of the essence of being. Positionality is the complete forgetting of the truth of being. The same, the self-differentiated essence of being, is of its own accord in a contrariety, and indeed in the way that the world surreptitiously ousts itself into positionality. Positional-ity, however, not only sets itself apart from the concealed worlding of the world, but rather, ordering all that presences into the standing reserve, positionality importunes upon the world with the completion of the forgetting of its worlding. Importuning in this way,[12] positionality sets after the truth of the essence of being with forgetfulness. This pursuit [*Nach-stellen*] is the authentic positioning [*Stellen*], which takes place in the essence of positionality. In this pursuit[13] there first rests that positioning of positionality that, in the manner of the ordering of the standing reserve, places all that presences into

---

11. only possible insofar as positionality is the event of appropriation

12. too one-sidedly viewed in terms of world

13. the word is here used differently than in theory and observation, although not without relation to these

the state of the unguardedness of the thing. The innermost essence of positioning, as which positionality essences, is pursuit as here characterized.

In Old High German, to pursue is called *fara*. The positioning gathered in itself as pursuit is the danger [*die Gefahr*]. The basic trait of the essence of danger is pursuit. Insofar as being as positionality pursues itself with the forgetting of its essence, beyng as beyng is the danger of its own essence. Thought from the essence of positionality and in regard to the refusal of world and the unguarding of the thing, beyng is the danger.[14] Beyng is unqualifiedly in itself, from itself, for itself, the danger. As this pursuit, which pursues its own essence with the forgetting of this essence, beyng as beyng is the danger. This essential danger is the way that what is same—world and positionality as the respective differentiation of what essences of beyng—displaces itself from itself in setting after itself. The thought that beyng in itself would essence as the danger of itself still remains strange for us and, because strange, all too easily misconstrued. For we only think what has been said in an essentially correct manner when we consider this: Beyng, thought from the essence of the pursuing positionality, is in no way equipped with the character of being dangerous, but rather the reverse: Beyng, as it has hitherto unfolded itself in metaphysics from the idea up to now and in accordance with its hitherto concealed essence, belongs to the danger that now reigns over beyng.

The danger is the collected pursuit as which positionality pursues the self-refusal of world with the forgetting of its truth through the unguarding of the thing.

The essence of technology is positionality. The essence of positionality is the danger. Beyng is, in its essence, the danger of itself. Only because it is the danger so construed is the danger in itself at the same time something dangerous for the human thinking of being. The zone of this dangerousness of the danger, which thinking must traverse in order to experience the essence of beyng, is that which earlier in another place was named errancy, with the provision that the error would not be a failure of knowledge, but rather would belong to the essence of truth in the sense of the unconcealment of

---

14. reversed

being.[15] The essence of errancy rests in the essence of beyng as the danger.

In this regard, what is most dangerous in the danger consists in the danger concealing itself as the danger that it is. Pursuing the essence of beyng, positionality dissembles its essential danger. Thus it comes to pass that, initially and long thereafter, we largely take no notice of this essence of beyng, essencing in itself as the danger of the truth of its essence, and if we ever do then only with difficulty.

We experience the danger not yet as the danger. We do not experience positionality as the self-pursuing and thus self-dissembling essence of being. Within the predominant relationship to being, we experience in being itself nothing of its essential danger, even though beings are everywhere permeated with dangers and distresses. Instead of referring us to the danger in the essence of being, the perils and plights precisely blind us to the danger. What is most dangerous in all this lies in the fact that the danger does not show itself as danger. It appears as though being itself would be innocuous and in itself dangerless since, on the one hand, being is ever still and only the most universal and emptiest of concepts, and what is more harmless than an empty concept? And since, on the other hand, being is the same as that most extant of beings, God.[16]

The danger, which takes place as the essence of positionality in the dominance of technology, reaches its culmination when in the midst of this singular danger there is everywhere only the innocuous, proliferating in the form of numerous accidental plights.

---

15. Translator's Note: See the 1930 lecture, first delivered in Bremen and published in 1943, "On the Essence of Truth," section 7, "Un-Truth as Errancy," now in Martin Heidegger, *Wegmarken*, 3rd ed., *Gesamtausgabe* vol. 9, ed. Friedrich-Wilhelm von Herrmann (Frankfurt a.M.: Vittorio Klostermann, 1996), 177–202, 196–98. English translation: "On the Essence of Truth," trans. John Sallis, in *Pathmarks*, ed. William McNeill, trans. various (Cambridge: Cambridge University Press, 1998), 136–54, 150–52.

16. Assuming however that God would be, surely not beyng itself, but the most extant being, then who today would dare to claim that, so conceived, God would be the danger for beyng?

As a consequence of every danger, a distress makes the rounds. Distress necessitates. It compels into the clueless, compels into despair. Admittedly, where *the* danger conceals itself, *the* distress likewise veils itself. Distress is thereby not experienced as distress. To be sure, one comes across a multitude of distresses and tribulations. One remedies them and alleviates them from case to case, first from a readiness to help that, through discreet acts, leaves no means untried and thus ameliorates the manifold suffering and assuages the distresses. Nonetheless, one does not attend to *the* distress. In relation to *the* distress, in the midst of the most extreme distress of the highest danger, distresslessness presides. In truth, though in a concealed manner, distresslessness is the authentic distress.

Everyone has their distresses. No one stands in *the* distress; for *the* danger does not appear to exist. Are there times when we could have noticed *the* distress, the dominance of distress-lessness? There are indications. Only we do not attend to them.

Hundreds of thousands die in masses. Do they die? They perish. They are put down. Do they die? They become pieces of inventory of a standing reserve for the fabrication of corpses. Do they die? They are unobtrusively liquidated in annihilation camps. And even apart from such as these—millions now in China abjectly end in starvation.

To die, however, means to carry out death in its essence. To be able to die means to be capable of carrying this out. We are only capable of it, however, when our essence is endeared to the essence of death.

Indeed in the midst of these innumerable dead, the essence of death remains disguised. Death is neither the empty nothing, nor is it merely the transition from one existence to another. *Death belongs in the Dasein of the human as appropriated from the essence of beyng.* Thus death harbors [*birgt*] the essence of beyng. Death is the highest refuge [*Gebirg*] of the truth of beyng itself, the refuge that in itself shelters [*birgt*] the concealment [*Verborgenheit*] of the essence of beyng and gathers together the sheltering [*Bergung*] of its essence. Thus the human is first and only capable of death when beyng itself from the truth of its essence brings the essence of the human into the ownership of the essence of beyng. *Death is the refuge of beyng in the poem of the world.* To be capable of death in its essence means to be able to die.

Those that are able to die are first of all the mortals in the weighty sense of this word. Massive distresses innumerable, horrific undying death all about—and nevertheless the essence of death is disguised from the human. The human is not yet the mortal.

Immeasurable suffering creeps and rages over the earth. The flood of suffering rises ever higher. But the essence of pain is concealed. Pain is the rift in which the basic sketch of the fourfold of the world is inscribed. From this basic sketch, that magnitude that is too great for humans receives its greatness. In the rift of pain, what is granted on high guards its perseverance. The rift of pain rends the veiled procession of grace into an unneeded arrival of favor. Everywhere we are assailed by innumerable and measureless suffering. We however are unpained, not brought into the ownership of the essence of pain.

A grizzly abjection makes the rounds. The army of the poor grows and grows. But the essence of poverty is concealed. What takes place in poverty is that what is simple and ameliorating of everything essential, this inconspicuously becomes a propriety [*Eigentum*] wherein the things enjoy dwelling in a granted world.

Death, the refuge of beyng, pain, the basic sketch of beyng, poverty, the release into the propriety of beyng, are all indications by which the danger lets it be noted that *the* distress remains outstanding in the midst of the tremendous distresses, that *the* danger does not *exist* as the danger. The danger is concealed in that it is disguised by positionality. This itself is veiled once again in what it lets essence, technology. This is also why our relationship to the essence of technology is so strange. To what extent is it strange? Because the essence of technology comes to light as nothing other than positionality, and the essence of this as nothing other than the danger, and this as nothing other than beyng itself. For this reason, precisely now, where everything indeed is more and more permeated by technological manifestations and the effects of technology, we everywhere still misinterpret technology. We think about it either too briefly or too hastily.

Specifically, we could now be tempted to summarily refute what has been discussed regarding technology, regarding positionality and the danger, in the following way: that technology would be a danger; nowadays this is proclaimed everywhere urgently and loudly enough. Many go even further in their judgment. One proclaims that technology would be a disaster for high culture; it wrenches everything away into mere civilization. One says technology would be the catastrophe of the modern world, the certain downfall of which is gauged by the unremitting dominance of technology.

Such judgments today are at one moment exclaimed passionately and warningly, at another expressed timidly and despondently. They determine in their many varieties the current opinion concerning technology, notwithstanding that at the same time one greedily scurries after the latest technological advance, perhaps even must so hurry after it. But it counts for nothing that here one's judgment and bearing in relation to technology are contradictory and that this contradiction could count as an objection. What is there that is actual in our Dasein that does not contradict itself? And yet this is perhaps even more actual than sheer logical consistency. We now pay heed to the judgments concerning technology just mentioned only in regards to how they conceive technology. They do not observe technology in regard to its essence and the provenance of this. They observe technology much more with an eye to its effect in relation to everything actual, by which one means that the actual would be found on its own outside of the essential region of technology: in culture, politics, morals, religion. One reckons how technology, supposedly one actuality among others, concerns all remaining actualities. One pursues technology, how it challenges forth the remaining actualities, how it positions them, assaults them with conscription, and thereby conducts them into utility or damages and disfigures them. One observes technology technologically. To be sure, this manner of observation corresponds to technology; it already places itself under the power of technological evaluation. But in so doing even technological judgments about technology never arrive at the essence of technology. They so little attain this that from the outset they even obstruct the way to the essential realm of technology. The said positions have never considered the essence of technology. And because their utterances do not speak from there, they remain external assessments. Thus it changes nothing if one abhors technology as disaster or prizes it as the greatest advance of humankind and extols it as the redeemer of humanity. The bearing to technology remains confused and thus at variance with itself. Without risking the step of thinking that exposes our human essence to the essence of technology (not only to its manipulations and uses), one struggles through these conflicts from case to case, situation to situation. And precisely through this mess one misses the possibility for which one in principle strives, the mastering of technology through human action and the directing of it in a manner befitting humans. But how is this supposed to ever be able to occur for all humanity, in the grand style, and in a historical sense, so long as the question concerning the essence of technology and its essential relation to the human essence has not even once been taken seriously? As long as we do not yet notice in the least bit that we must first thoughtfully enter into and open up the essential region of technology in order to then act and reflect within this essential space in an expressly technological manner, that is how long we will not be able to find any befitting decisions concerning technology.

Yet there are indeed doctrines concerning technology that pronounce it to be neither something evil nor something good. One says technology would be neutral, everything depends on what the human does with technology and makes of it; everything would rest upon whether the human is in a position to take technology by the hand and is willing to assign technology to loftier goals; everything would be decided by this, whether the human is able to master technology morally and religiously or not.

No one will deny the seriousness of the responsibility in this position on technology. And nevertheless, even this consideration of technology thinks technology just as little in its essence as the previous ones, for whoever presumes technology to be something neutral first rightly conceives it merely as an instrument by which something else is effected and arranged. Whoever takes technology as something neutral conceives it once again only instrumentally, and that means technologically. Indeed, technology does not consist in the technological, but only conceals its essence there.

The essence of technology is itself nothing technological. Admittedly, for those who hold technology to be something neutral, there arises the misleading appearance as though they observed technology directly in an objective manner, even in itself, which is to say, free from every evaluation. To be sure, this appearance is deceptive. One may hold technology for something devilish or for something godly or for something neutral, but with all these conceptions and valuations one is from the outset unwittingly in agreement that technology would be a means to an end. Technology taken as a means is placed in the hand of the human. Technology conceived as a means counts as one actuality among many other actualities. Whoever takes technology as a means, wittingly or unwittingly, in any case surely appears to evaluate it positively and to accomplish a worthy confrontation with it. In truth, however, wherever technology is taken instrumentally as a means or even as a tool, it is degraded in its essence. It is held to be some being among many other beings, while indeed being itself essences in and as technology. If on the contrary a thinking attempts to experience the essence of technology in the reigning gathering of a universal positioning, that is, in positionality thought in this manner, then, in a way, there lies in such a thinking the unspoken claim of dignifying the essence of technology. Within contemporary thinking, such a dignifying can scarcely be surpassed. The usual opinions concerning technology are by no means mentioned here in order to enumerate how they refrain from thinking or to decry that they nowhere reach into the essence of technology, or even to contradict them as false judgments. All this opining concerning technology, presiding in many varieties and historically necessary, is mentioned now solely because in so doing it becomes clear how the dominance of the essence of technology orders into its plundering even and especially the human conceptions concerning technology.

The essential violence of technology does not first of all lie in the effect of high-frequency machines, but rather in that technology, proximally and for the most part, only presents itself to human representation technologically. The essence of technology, positionality, conducts its own disguising.

One is also relinquished to this self-disguising of positionality when, at times, one darkly gleans and clearly admits for a moment that technology has long withdrawn from mere application as a means and that, to the contrary, technology itself now would much more draw the human after it as its instrument, be it that the human blindly follows this wresting away, be it that he unflaggingly strives to put technology to healing and beneficial purposes. The human is even relinquished to the riddlesome self-concealing of the essence of technology when he avows that, in the end, technology would indeed be something more and something other than a means in the hand of the human.

But it is not only in the end that technology is no longer a mere instrument, but rather from its essential beginning onward it has never been a means in the hand of the human. From the outset, it has withdrawn from its treatment as a means, although the everyday appearance of technological accomplishments and effects proffers something else.

Indeed when one confusedly intimates here and there that technology could, in truth, be something other than a means, one does so with the help of grand-sounding but unthought words, and only thus draws oneself out of the influence of a dark compulsion that has befallen the human essence from the essence of technology itself. One says technology would be something demonic. One says this demonism of technology would bring the willing and acting of the human into a tragic entanglement. In so needy a time as ours, one should not drag out words that stem from the language of a great thinking age, where precisely what is loftily thought, and only this, lights up and guards the realm of appearance for the gods, the δαίμονες, and fate, τύχη. The helpless terror before what is supposedly demonic in technology and its supposedly tragic consequences is in truth anxiety before a thinking that considers what *is,* a thinking that, outside the artifice and acumen of the intellect, but also without sentimentality, soberly seeks its path in what is to be thought. Technology is in its essence neither a means to an end, nor is it itself an end. Its essence reigns outside of the realm of ends and means, a realm that is determined by causal effects [*ursächliche Wirken*] and thus circumscribed as the realm of the actual [*des Wirklichen*]. Technology in its essence is not at all something actual alongside other actualities. It is the concealed basic trait of the actuality of everything now actual. The basic trait of actuality is presence. Presencing belongs in the essence of being itself. The essence of technology is beyng itself in the essential form of positionality. The essence of positionality, however, is *the danger*. But let us consider it clearly: Positionality is not the danger because it is the essence of technology and because threatening and dangerous effects can arise from technology. The danger is positionality, not as technology, but rather as beyng. What essences of danger is beyng itself insofar as it pursues the truth of its essence with the forgetting of this essence. Because the essence of technology is nothing less than beyng itself; the essence of technology has been named with the bewildering name "positionality."

Having considered in a few strokes the issue of the essence of technology as the being of contemporary beings, a few things can likewise now briefly be said concerning the name for this essence of technology, concerning the word "positionality."

The word "to position, place, set" [*stellen*] corresponds to the Greek θέσις, assuming that we think θέσις in a Greek manner. What does it mean in this case to "think in a Greek manner"? It means: attending to which illuminated clearing of the essence of beyng it is that has laid claim to the Dasein of the Ancient Greeks and to the way in which it has done so; it means considering from the outset under which dispensation of which unconcealment of being the Greeks stood, for according to the claim of this dispensation their language spoke and every word of this language so speaks. Such attention to the Greek is a little more difficult than the pursuits of classical philology. Such attention is thus even more exposed to the possibility of error than the latter science. To think in a Greek manner does not mean to conduct oneself merely according to the doctrines of classical philology. If it only meant this, we would run the danger that thinking and what is to be thought would be delivered over to a historiological representing that, as a science, lives by not acknowledging its specious presuppositions. What does the word θέσις say when we think it in a Greek manner? θέσις means positioning, placing, setting [*stellen*]. This positioning corresponds to Φύσις, so much so that it is defined by Φύσις, within the region of Φύσις, and from its relation to Φύσις. This points out that within Φύσις itself a certain θέσις-character is concealed. In the Greek world a chief distinction was expressed by the words φύσει and θέσει. It concerns what presences as such in the way that it presences. The distinction concerns the presencing of what presences, i.e., it concerns being. θέσει, θέσις is accordingly thought in relation to being. Thus the relationship between being and positioning was already announced in the first epoch of the history of being. If we attend to this, then from the outset it can no longer bewilder us if once in a subsequent epoch being itself takes place in the manner of a positioning in the sense of positionality. Thereby, and this is something that needs to be repeatedly impressed upon us, we must think positionality [*Ge-Stell*] as corresponding to growth [*Gewächs*] and indeed growth as the gathering of what grows [*des Wachstums*]. Positionality: the gathering of positioning in the sense of pursuing and requisitioning as previously indicated. It is not bewildering that the essence of being attains an essential relation with positioning; what is bewildering is only that for centuries one has never inquired into this relationship. In what sense and in which way is it already shown at the dawn of the destiny of being that a θέσις-character essences in being, i.e., in Φύσις?

Φύσις says: the self-clearing emergence from itself, which brings forth from concealment here into unconcealment that which emergently presences. Φύσις is the bringing-here-forth [*Her-vor-bringen*], clearing and emerging from itself. But here we cannot understand the word "bringing-here-forth" in the inexact and all-too-common meaning [to produce, beget], where it seems to not require any explication. Much more must we think bringing-here-forth rigorously in the unified dimension that joins concealment (Λήθη) and unconcealment ('Α-λήθεια), while relating each of these to the other in accordance with their essence, that is, guarding each of them reciprocally in their essence. Bringing-here-forth, thought in a Greek manner in the sense of Φύσις, means to bring here from concealment forth into unconcealment. This bringing means letting something arrive and presence of its own accord.[17] Only when Φύσις reigns is θέσις possible and necessary. For only when there is something present that is brought about by a bringing-here-forth can human positioning, θέσις, then arrange upon such a presence (i.e., the stone) and out of this presence (stone) now something else that presences (a stone

---

17. Λόγος: to bring-to-lie-before, letting-lie-before

staircase and its steps), here among what is already present (the native rocks and soil). What now presences (the stone staircase) presences in the manner of something that, through human positioning (θέσις), i.e., production [*Herstellen*], becomes steady. *What stands here through* θέσις *essences otherwise than what is brought forth here by* φύσις. All the same, it is common to conceive even that which is brought here and brought forth in Φύσις, and thus that which presences, as something standing here. What is brought here forth in Φύσις is standing here [*herständig*] in unconcealment not through a human production,[18] but rather through a bringing-here-forth of itself from itself. Bringing in the manner of Φύσις is now a positioning along-side, a positioning that sets up in unconcealment that which presences from itself. Φύσις, setting itself up in the uncon-cealed, is the letting presence of what presences in unconceal-ment.[19] The letting presence of what presences is the being of beings. So construed, Φύσις, the emerging bringing-here-forth from itself, showed itself from early on to bear the character of a positioning that is not a human accomplishment. On the contrary Φύσις first brings what presences as such to human production and representation by simultaneously giving un-concealment to humans and placing it at their disposal. Thus, by bringing and giving, it delivers a shelter in unconcealment. But this positioning, the bringing-here-forth from itself of a letting persevere and a sheltering, still has nothing of those traits that the essence of beyng shows in its destiny, which it appropriates[20] as positionality. All the same, positioning es-sences in the manner of a pursuing-ordering positionality, from a concealed provenance in—and an essential relatedness to—positioning in the sense of Φύσις.

The word "positionality" names the essence of technology. Technology does not essence in the manner of a requisitioning and pursuing due to the technological process of building and using an apparatus, something that still appears to us as a "framework" [*Gestell*] in the sense of scaffolding and equipment. The essence of technology bears the name positionality because

18. ποίησις
19. "Bringing-near"; the "essence" of presence persevering [An-"wesen" währen]
20. ambiguous!

the positioning that is named in positionality is being itself [*das Sein selber*], but beyng at the beginning of its destiny had illuminated itself as Φύσις, as the self-emergent delivering that brings-here-forth. From this essence of beyng, from Φύσις, beyng in its essencing as positionality has received its name as a fief.

The essential genealogy of positionality as the essence of technology reaches into and shows the essential provenance of the Western-European and, today, planetary destiny of being from Φύσις. It is a dispensation in which the unconcealment of presencing, as the veiled inceptual essence of being, makes its address. Since the early days of the Greeks this claim is no longer silenced. It has most recently spoken in what Nietzsche uttered as the will to power, essencing in the eternal recurrence of the same [*des Gleichen*]. What the thinker says of being is not his opinion. What is said is the echo speaking through him of the claim that essences as beyng itself in that It brings itself to language.

To be an echo is more difficult and more rare than to have opinions and to represent standpoints. To be an echo is the suffering of thinking. This passion is a quiet sobriety. It is infinitely more difficult, because more endangered, than the highly touted objectivity of scientific research. To be an echo, namely of the claim of being, requires a carefulness with language that the technical-terminological style of language in the sciences can know nothing of at all. The internationality of scientific language is the starkest proof of its uprootedness from the soil and lack of homeland, though this by no means says that rootedness in the soil and what is homely of language would be in the least bit guaranteed, determined, or even founded by what is merely national. What is homely in a high language thrives only in the region of the uncanny claim of an essential stillness in the essence of beyng.

The name positionality, spoken to technology and thoughtfully heard by it, says that its essence determines an epoch of beyng because its essence, positioning, rests in the inceptual destiny of beyng (Φύσις-Θέσις). The Θέσις concealed in the essence of Φύσις at the dawn of the destiny of beyng, i.e., positioning, comes properly to language in the later epochs of the modern dispensation of being, there where Kant, a pure echo of the claim of the being of beings concernfully approaching him, pronounced the essence of being as "absolute position," as the positedness and positionhood of the object, i.e., of what presences.[21]

Positionality—spoken as the thoughtful name of the essence of technology and not as the otherwise current word, named superficially with the derogatory tone of something adverse— says: technology is no mere product of culture and no mere manifestation of civilization. According to its essence, technology, reigning of its own accord, is the gathering of positioning in the sense of a requisitioning into standing reserve of all that presences. The basic characteristic of this ordering positioning, however, essences in that pursuit in which beyng itself pursues its own essence with the forgetting of this essence.[22] Beyng itself essences, insofar as it turns away from its essence, in that it turns to this essence with the forgetfulness of it.

---

21. but posited by whom? the human subject? by what right? Translator's Note: Cf. Immanuel Kant, "Der einzig mögliche Beweisgrund zu einer Demonstration des Dasein Gottes," in *Vorkritische Schriften II: 1757–1777*, vol. 2 of *Kants gesammelte Schriften*, ed. Königlich Preußischen Akademie der Wissenschaften (Berlin: Georg Reimer, 1912), 63–163, 73. English translation: Immanuel Kant, "The only possible argument in support of a demonstration of the existence of God," in *Theoretical Philosophy 1755–1770*, ed. and trans. David Walford with Ralf Meerbote (Cambridge: Cambridge University Press, 1992), 107–201, 119.

22. Why? How to think this from the event of appropriation?

The Turn

The essence of positionality is the collected positioning that pursues its own essential truth with forgetfulness, a pursuit disguised in that it unfolds in the requisitioning of everything that presences as standing reserve, establishing itself in this and ruling as this.

Positionality essences as the danger. But does the danger already exist *as* the danger? No. Perils and distresses immeasurably press upon humans everywhere at every hour. But the danger, namely beyng itself in the self-endangering truth of its essence, remains veiled and disguised. This disguising is what is most dangerous about the danger. Through this disguising of the danger in the requisitioning of positionality it always appears ever again as though technology were a means in the hand of the human. In truth, however, the essence of the human is now ordered to give a hand to the essence of technology.

Does this say that the human is powerless against technology and delivered over to it for better or worse? No. It says exactly the opposite; not only this, but essentially more, because it says something other than this.

If positionality is an essential destiny of beyng itself, then we may suppose that, as one essential way of beyng among others, positionality changes. For what is destinal in the dispensation is that it sends itself each time in a sending. To send oneself [*sich schicken*, to be fitting, suitable; to reconcile oneself with] means to set out to comply with the indicated directive, upon which another still-veiled dispensation awaits. In itself, the destinal goes forth each time to an exceptional moment, which it sends in another dispensation, though without simply

64

going under and getting lost in this. We are still too inexperienced and rash to think the essence of the destinal in terms of
dispensation, sending, and compliance. We are still too easily
inclined, because accustomed, to conceive the dispensational
[*das Geschickliche*] in terms of what happens [*dem Geschehen*]
and to represent this as a course of historiologically determin-
able incidents. We place history in the realm of what occurs,
instead of thinking history in accordance with its essential
provenance in terms of destiny. Destiny, however, is essentially
the dispensation of being, so much so that being itself sends
itself and each time essences as a dispensation and destinally
transforms itself in accordance with this. When a change in
being takes place, i.e., as it does now in the essence of positionality, then this by no means says that technology, whose
essence rests in positionality, would be abolished. It is neither
struck down nor smashed apart.

If the essence of technology, positionality as the danger in
beyng, is beyng itself, then technology can never be mastered
by a mere human action alone, whether positive or negative.
Technology, whose essence is being itself, can never be overcome by the human. That would indeed mean that the human
would be the master of being.

Yet since beyng has sent itself as the essence of technology in
positionality, and since the human *essence* belongs to the essence
of beyng insofar as the essence of beyng needs the human essence, in accordance with its own essence, in order to remain
guarded in the midst of beings as being, and thus needs it in
order to essence as beyng, then for this reason the essence of
technology cannot be led to a transformation of its destiny without the assistance of the human essence. Thereby technology is
not humanly overcome; much to the contrary, the essence of
technology is converted into its still-concealed truth. This conversion is similar to what occurs when, in the human realm, a
pain is converted. Yet the conversion of a dispensation of being,
here and now the conversion of positionality, every time takes
place through the arrival of another dispensation, which can be
neither logically-historiologically predicted nor metaphysically
construed as the result of a process of history. For the dispensation is never determined by something historical, and especially
not by the historiologically conceived occurrence, but rather

every time what occurs is already something destinal from a dispensation of beyng.

For the conversion of the essence of technology, the human is nevertheless needed; but the human is here needed in his essence, as it corresponds to this conversion. Accordingly, the essence of the human must first open itself to the essence of technology, which is an entirely different event than the process by which humans affirm and further technology and its means. But in order that the human essence would become attentive to the essence of technology, in order that an essential relationship would be founded between technology and the human in respect to their essences, the modern human must first of all find his way back into the breadth of his essential space. The dimension that joins together this essential space of the human essence is only received through that relationship by which the guardianship of beyng itself is brought into the ownership of the human essence as what is needed by it. Apart from first cultivating himself within this essential space and taking up a dwelling therein, the human is not capable of anything essential within the dispensation now reigning. In considering this, we attend to a saying of Meister Eckhart and think it from its ground. It runs: "Those who are not of great essence, whatever work they effect, nothing will come of it."[1]

The great essence of the human lies in its belonging to the essence of being. It is needed by the essence of being so as to guard it in its truth. For this it is above all necessary that we first consider the essence of being as thought-worthy, first experience such thinking, and that by such an experience first trace a path and make our way into the hitherto impassable.

We are capable of all this only if, in regards to what seems to be the question that is always closest and solely urgent—what are we to do?—we first and only consider this: How must we

---

1. Meister Eckhart, *Meister Eckharts Reden der Unterscheidung*, no. 4, ed. Ernst Diederichs, anastatic reprint of the 1913 edition (Bonn: A. Marcus und E. Weber Verlag, 1925), 8–9, 8. Meister Eckhart, "Reden der Unterscheidung," no. 4, in *Die deutschen Werke*, vol. 5: *Meister Eckharts Traktate*, ed. and trans. Josef Quint (Stuttgart: Kohlhammer, 1963), 196–98, 198. English translation: "Those in whom being is but slight, whatever deeds they do amount to nothing," from "The Talks of Instruction," no. 4, in Eckhart, *Complete Mystical Works*, 489, 489.

think, for thinking is the authentic action [*Handeln*], where action means to give a hand [*an die Hand gehen*] to the essence of beyng in order to prepare for it that site in which it brings itself and its essence to speech. Without language, all will to contemplation remains without any path or route. Without language, every deed lacks any dimension in which it could move about and have effect. Language is thus never merely the expression of thinking, feeling, and willing. Language is the inceptual dimension within which the human essence is first capable of corresponding to being and its claim and of belonging to being through this correspondence. This inceptual correspondence, properly enacted, is thinking. By thinking we first learn to dwell in the realm in which the conversion of the dispensation of being, the conversion of positionality, takes place.

The essence of positionality is the danger. As danger, being turns away from its essence into the forgetfulness of this essence and thus at the same time turns itself against the truth of its essence. This self-turning that has not yet been considered reigns in the danger. In the essence of danger there is concealed the possibility of a turn in which the forgetting of the essence of being so turns that through this turn the truth of the essence of beyng properly enters into beings.

Presumably, however, this turn from the forgetting of being to the guardianship of the essence of beyng only takes place when the danger, pivotal in its concealed essence, first properly presences as the danger that it is. Perhaps we already stand in the shadows cast in advance of this turn's arrival. When and how this will dispensationally take place, no one knows. It is also not necessary to know such a thing. A knowledge of this sort would even be most fatal for the human because his essence is to be the one waiting, the one who waits upon the essence of beyng by protecting it in thinking. Only when the human as the shepherd of being waits for the truth of beyng can he at all expect—and without deteriorating into a mere wanting to know—the arrival of another dispensation of being.

But what about when the danger takes place as the danger and thus is first unconcealed as the danger? In order to hear the answer to this question, let us attend to the hint that is preserved in a word of Hölderlin's. In the later version of the hymn "Patmos" the poet says at the beginning:

But where the danger is, there grows
also what saves.[2]

Let us think this saying even more essentially than the poet
poetized it, let us think it through to its most extreme, for
then it says:
   Where the danger is as danger, that which saves is already
there. The latter does not insert itself alongside the former.
What saves does not stand next to the danger. When it is as the
danger, the danger itself is what saves. The danger is what saves
insofar as, from out of its essence, it brings what saves. What
does "to save" mean? It says: to let loose, to disengage, to free
[*freyen*], to spare, to shelter, to take under protection, to guard.
Lessing still uses the word "salvation" [*Rettung*] in an emphatic
manner with the sense of justification: to restore something to
its right, the essential, and to guard it therein.[3] What genuinely
saves is what guards, guardianship.
   But where is the danger? What is the place for it? Insofar as
the danger is beyng itself, it is nowhere and everywhere. It has
no place. It itself is the placeless location of everything that
presences. The danger is the epoch of beyng, essencing as
positionality.
   If the danger is as the danger, then its essence properly takes
place. But the danger is the pursuit by which beyng itself, in the
manner of positionality, sets after the guardianship of beyng
with forgetfulness. What essences in pursuit is that beyng

---

2. Friedrich Hölderlin, "Patmos," in *Sämtliche Werke,* historisch-kritische
Ausgabe, vol. 4: *Gedichte 1800–1806,* 2nd ed., ed. Norbert von Hellingrath
(Berlin: Propyläen Verlag, 1923), 227–30, 227. English translation:
Friedrich Hölderlin, "Patmos," in *Poems & Fragments,* ed. and trans. Michael
Hamburger, 3rd ed. (London: Anvil Press Poetry, 1994), 483–97, 483,
translation modified.
3. Translator's Note: Lessing titled a series of short essays in defense of
forgotten or condemned figures in the history of ideas *"Rettungen"* or *"Vin-
dications."* See, for example, the *"Rettungen des Horaz," "Rettung des Hier.
Cardanus," "Rettung des* Inepti Religiosi *und seines ungennanten* Verfassers,"
and the *"Rettung des Cochläus aber nur in einer Kleinigkeit,"* in Gotthold
Ephraim Lessing, *Sämtliche Schriften,* ed. Karl Lachmann and Franz
Muncker, vol. 5 (Stuttgart: G. J. Göschen'sche Verlagshandlung, 1890;
reprinted, Berlin: Walter de Gruyter, 1968), 272–367.

displaces its truth into forgetfulness such that beyng refuses its essence. Consequently, if the danger is as the danger, then the pursuit properly takes place whereby beyng itself pursues its truth with forgetfulness. When this pursuit with forgetting properly takes place, then forgetting as such makes an entrance. Torn out of its lapsing by this entrance, it is no longer forgetfulness. Through such an entrance, the forgetfulness of the guardianship of beyng is no longer the forgetting of beyng, but by entering it turns into the guardianship of beyng. When the danger is as the danger then, along with the turn of forgetting, the guardianship of beyng takes place, the world takes place. That the world would take place as world, that the thing would thing, this is the distant arrival of the essence of beyng itself.

The self-refusal of the truth of beyng, pursuing itself with forgetfulness, harbors a still-ungranted grace: that this self-pursuit turn itself, that through such a turn forgetfulness turn itself about and become guardianship of the essence of beyng, instead of letting this essence lapse into dissemblance. In the essence of danger there essences and dwells a grace, namely the grace of the turn of the forgetting of beyng into the truth of beyng. In the essence of danger, where it is as the danger, there is the turn to guardianship, there is this guardianship itself, there is that which saves of beyng [*das Rettende des Seyns*].

When the turn takes place in the danger, this can only occur without mediation. For beyng has nothing similar to itself next to it. It is not effected by another, nor does it take effect. Beyng never runs through a causal network of effects. As beyng, the way that beyng sends itself neither precedes anything effected, nor follows upon anything causative. Abruptly from out of its own essence of concealment, beyng takes place in its epoch. Thus we must take note: The turn of the danger takes place suddenly. In the turn there suddenly lights up the illuminated clearing of the essence of beyng. This sudden self-lighting is the lightning flash. It brings itself into the brightness proper to it, a brightness it brought in with itself. In the turn of the danger, when the truth of beyng flashes, the essence of beyng lights up; the truth of the essence of beyng enters. In taking place, toward what does the entrance *(doorway)* [*Einkehr*] turn? Toward nothing other than beyng itself, essencing as yet in the forgetfulness of its truth. But this beyng itself essences as the essence of technology. The essence of technology is positionality. The entrance, as event of the turn of forgetting, enters into what is now the epoch of beyng. That which is, is in no way this or that being. What authentically is—and this means properly dwelling and essencing in the Is—is solely beyng. Only beyng "is," only in beyng and as beyng does there take place what the "is" names; that which is, is beyng from out of its essence.

"To flash" [*blitzen*], according to the word and the issue at stake, is to glance [*blicken*]. In the glance [*im Blick*] and as the glance, what is essencing enters into its own illumination. Through the element of its illumination, the glance shelters back in the glancing whatever it catches sight of; at the same time, glancing likewise guards in illumination the hidden darkness of its provenance as what is unilluminated. Entrance [*Einkehr*] of the lightning flash of the truth of being is insight [*Einblick*]. We thought the truth of beyng in the worlding of world as the mirror-play of the fourfold of sky and earth, mortals and divinities. When forgetfulness turns, when the world as guardian of the essence of beyng makes its entrance, there takes place the flashing entry [*Einblitz*] of world into the unguarding of the thing. This takes place in the manner of the dominance of positionality. The flashing entry of the world in positionality is the flashing entry of the truth of beyng into unguarded being [*das wahrlose Sein*]. Flashing entry is the event of appropriation in beyng itself.

Insight into that which is—this title now names the event of the turn in beyng, the turn from the refusal of its essence into the event of its guardianship.[4] Insight into that which is is the appropriative event itself, as which the truth of beyng relates itself to unguarded beyng and stands by it. Insight into that which is—this names the constellation in the essence of beyng. This constellation is the dimension in which beyng essences as the danger. At first and almost to the very end it appeared as though "insight into that which is" signified only a glance that we humans cast forth from ourselves to that which is. "That which is" one customarily takes as a particular being, for indeed the "is" is said of beings. But now everything has turned. Insight does not

---

4. relationship [*Ver-Hältnis*]

name our inspection of the being, insight as flashing entry is the appropriative event of the constellation of the turn in the essence of beyng itself in the epoch of positionality. By no means is that which is the being. For the "it is" and the "is" are only avowed of the being insofar as the being is addressed in respect to its being. "Being" is uttered in the "is"; that which is, in the sense that it constitutes the being of beings, is being.

The requisitioning of positionality places itself before the thing, leaving it unguarded as thing, truthless. Thus positionality disguises the nearing nearness of the world in the thing. Positionality even disguises this, its disguising, just as the forgetting of something is itself forgotten and drawn away in the wake of forgetfulness. The event of forgetfulness does not only allow a lapse into concealment, but rather this lapsing itself lapses into concealment along with it, which itself even falls away with this fall.

And nevertheless—in all this disguising of positionality, the glimmer of world still lights up, the truth of beyng flashes. Namely when positionality in its essence as the danger is lit up. Even in positionality as an essential destiny of being there essences a light from the flash of beyng. Positionality, although veiled, is still a glance, not a blind destiny in the sense of a completely oppressive doom.

Insight into that which is—thus is named the lightning flash of the truth of beyng into truthless being.

When insight takes place then the humans are struck to their essence by the lightning flash of beyng. The humans are what is caught sight of in the insight.

Only when the human essence, as what is caught sight of in the appropriative event of insight, disavows human stubbornness and casts itself before this insight, throwing its stubbornness away, only then does the human correspond in his essence to the claim of the insight. The human is suited for corresponding in this way in that he looks toward the divinities as one of the mortals from the guarded element of the world. Other than this it does not happen; for even God, if he exists, is a being and as a being stands in beyng and its essence, which itself takes place from the worlding of the world.

Only when insight takes place does the essence of technology light up as positionality, do we recognize how the truth of beyng as world remains refused in the requisitioning of the standing reserve, do we remark that all mere willing and doing in the manner of requisitioning only perpetuates the unguarding. Likewise all mere ordering of the world as represented by universal historiology remains truthless and without purchase. All mere chasing of the future in order to calculate its image by extrapolating a half-thought present into what is veiled in its coming, this all still moves within the bearing of a technological-calculating conception. All attempts to reckon up the presiding actuality, whether morphologically, psychologically in terms of decay and loss, in terms of disaster and catastrophe, of downfall, are all only instances of a technological behavior. It acts through an apparatus for the enumeration of symptoms, the stock of which can be endlessly increased and varied ever anew. These analyses of the situation do not note that they only work in the sense and manner of a technological disassembly, and that they thus deliver to technological consciousness the historiological-technological presentation of what occurs in the manner that befits it. Yet no historiological conception of history as occurrence brings in the fitting [*schicklichen*] relation to destiny.

Everything merely technological never reaches into the essence of technology. It is not even capable of knowing its vestibule. Thus in attempting to say the insight into that which is, we are not describing the situation of the times. Rather, the constellation of beyng should speak to us.

But we do not yet hear it, we whose hearing and sight deteriorate under the dominance of technology by means of radio and film. The constellation of beyng is the refusal of world as the unguarding of the thing.[5] Refusal[6] is not nothing, it is the highest secret of beyng within the dominance of positionality.

Whether the God lives or remains dead is not decided by the religiosity of humans and even less by the theological aspirations of philosophy and natural science. Whether God is God, this takes place from and within the constellation of beyng. As long as we do not thoughtfully experience what is, we can never belong to what will be [*was seyn wird*].

Does the insight into that which is take place?

---

5. forgetting of the differentiation; language
6. relationship [*Ver-Hältnis*]

As what is caught sight of, will we be taken into the essential glance of beyng so that we no longer escape it? Do we thereby attain the essence of nearness, which, thinging in the thing, brings the world near? Do we dwell at home in nearness such that we inceptually belong in the fourfold of sky and earth, mortals and divinities?

Does the insight into that which is take place? Do we correspond to the insight by a glancing that glances into the essence of technology and perceives in it beyng itself?

Do we see the lightning flash of beyng in the essence of technology? The lightning flash that comes out of the stillness as this stillness itself? Stillness appeases. What does it appease? It appeases beyng in the essence of world.[7]

The world, worlding, would be the nearest of everything near that nears in that it brings the truth of beyng near to the human essence and thus brings the human into the ownership of the event of appropriation.

---

7. Language!

BASIC PRINCIPLES OF THINKING: FREIBURG LECTURES 1957

Lecture I

The basic principles of thinking guide and regulate the activity of thinking. They are therefore also named the laws of thought. One accords to them the principle of identity, the principle of contradiction, the principle of the excluded middle. According to common opinion the laws of thought are valid for all thinking, regardless of what is each time thought and independent of how the thinking then proceeds. The laws of thought require no regard for either the content of the objects each time considered or for the form, i.e., the kind of thought process. Empty of content, the laws of thought are mere forms. The constructing of concepts, the rendering of judgments, and the drawing of conclusions all move within these forms of thinking. The empty forms of thought can thus be formally presented. The principle of identity has the formula: $A = A$. The principle of contradiction states: $A \neq$ not A. The principle of the excluded middle requires: X is either A or not A.

The formulas for the laws of thought play into each other in a peculiar way. Thus there have also been attempts to derive them from each other. This occurred in various ways. The principle of contradiction, $A \neq$ not A, was represented as the negative form of the positive principle of identity, $A = A$. But also the reverse: Insofar as it rests upon a hidden contrariety, the principle of identity counts as the still-undeveloped form of the principle of contradiction. The principle of the excluded middle arises either as the immediate consequence of the first two or it is conceived as their intermediary. However one treats the laws of thought, they are held to be immediately obvious, one often even supposes that they would have to be so. For, viewed correctly, the fundamental principles cannot be proven. Indeed, every proof is already an act of thinking. The proof therefore already stands under the laws of thought. How could it presume to place itself above these in order to first justify their truth? But even if we hold the particular question of the provability or improvability of the laws of thought to be an unfitting one, the difficulty remains that in considering the rules of thought we get tangled up in a contradiction. We fall into an odd situation with the laws of thought. Namely, whenever we try to bring the basic principles of thinking before us they ineluctably become the topic of our thinking—and of its laws. Every time, the laws of thinking already stand behind us, behind our back, so to speak, and guide every step of our reflections concerning them. At first glance, this reference is illuminating. But with a single stroke it appears to undermine every attempt to appropriately consider the laws of thinking.

But this appearance dissipates as soon as we notice what befell the history of Western thinking. Historiologically calculated, the incident lies nearly one and a half centuries ago. The incident announced itself in that, through the efforts of the thinkers Fichte, Schelling, and Hegel, and as prepared for by Kant, thinking was brought into another dimension of its possibilities, in certain respects its highest. Thinking knowingly becomes dialectical. The poetic ponderings of Hölderlin and Novalis likewise move about within the purview of this dialectic, and are even more excitedly roused by its unfathomed depths. The theoretical-speculative development of the dialectic into a fully executed and enclosed domain is achieved in that work of Hegel's titled *The Science of Logic.*

The incident by which thinking enters the dimension of dialectic is a historical one. Consequently it appears to lie behind us. This appearance persists because we are accustomed to representing history historiologically. In the course of the following lectures our relationship to history will ever again play a role. Thus as a preview of this we note the following.

As long as we represent history historiologically, it appears as occurrences, these however in the sequence of a before and after. We find ourselves in a present through which what occurs flows away. Starting from here, on the basis of this present, the past is calculated. For it, the future is planned. The historiological representation of history as a sequence of occurrences prevents us from experiencing to what extent authentic history is constantly an impending [Gegen-wart] in an essential sense. By present [Gegenwart] here we do not mean what is directly present-at-hand in the momentary now. The impending [Gegen-wart] is what waits toward us [uns entgegenwartet], waits for whether and how we expose ourselves to it or, contrarily, close ourselves off from it. That which waits toward us also comes to us; it is the future [Zu-kunft], rightly thought. It pervades what is impending as an imposition [Zumutung] that approaches the Da-sein of the human, seeming [anmutet] to him in one way or another, so that he would surmise [vermute] the future in its claim. Only in the air of such surmising does questioning thrive, that essential questioning which belongs to the bringing forth of every genuine work in any field whatsoever.

A work is only a work in that it corresponds to the imposition of the future and thereby releases what has-been [das Gewesene] into its concealed essence, delivering it over to this. The great tradition comes to us as future. From the calculation of the past it never becomes what it is: imposition, claim. Just as every great work itself must first awaken and shape that human race that each time brings the world concealed in the work into its own space of freedom, so must the bringing forth of the work, for its part, listen ahead to the tradition addressed to it. What one is accustomed to calling the productive and ingenious character of a work does not stem from a welling up of feelings and inspirations from the unconscious; it is much more the alert obedience to history, an obedience that rests in the pure freedom of being able to hear.

Authentic history is an impending. What impends is the future as the imposition of the inceptual—i.e., of what is already enduring, essencing—as well as its concealed gathering. Impending is also the concernfully approaching claim of what has-been [des Gewesenen]. When one says that, basically, history brings nothing new, then this expression is untrue, provided it means that there would always only be the ever-same monotony. If, however, the statement "there is nothing new under the sun" says this: there is only what is old in the inexhaustible transformational violence of the inceptual, then the sentence hits upon the essence of history. It is the arrival of what has-been. It is this, what is already-essencing, and only this that comes to us. The past, however, recedes from us. For historiological calculation, history is what is past and the present is what is current. Yet the current remains the eternally futureless. We are flooded by historiology and only seldom find an insight into history. Newspaper, radio, television, and the paperback book industries are today the standard and planetary forms alike of the historiological calculation of the past, i.e., of its actualization in current events. It would be blindness if one wanted to do away with these processes, blindness, too, to blindly expedite them instead of considering them in their essence. For these processes belong to our history, in that which comes toward us.

We now also name as historical the incident by which thinking has entered into the dimension of dialectic.

What does this mean, that the dialectic would be a dimension? At first it remains unclear what dialectic is and what the talk of dimension employed here might mean. We are familiar with dimensions in terms of regions of space. Dimension can mean so much as extension: an industrial plant of great dimensions, i.e., size. But we also speak of the three-dimensional space familiar to us. As distinct from a line, a plane is another dimension. But the former is not merely stacked together into the latter; rather, in relation to the linear manifold, the plane takes this manifold up into itself. In so doing, it is another domain for a rule [*Maßgabe*] in regard to this manifold. The same holds for bodies in relation to the planar manifold. Bodies, planes, and lines each implicate a distinct rule. If we put aside the spatial restriction, then a dimension shows itself as the domain of a rule. Thus rules and domains are not two distinct or separate things, but rather one and the same. The rule each time yields and opens a domain wherein the rule is at home and can be what it is.

When we characterize the dialectic as a dimension of thinking and even have to recognize it as the highest dimension of thinking in the historical course of metaphysics, then this now says: By becoming dialectical, thinking reaches a previously closed-off domain of a rule for the delineation of its own essence. Through dialectics, thinking reaches a domain in which it is able to think itself completely. Thereby thinking first comes to itself. Within the dimension of the dialectic, it becomes evident in a founded manner that and how there belongs to thinking not only the possibility but the necessity of thinking itself, of mirroring itself in itself, of reflecting. In the dimension of dialectic there comes to light entirely for the first time why and in which way thinking is reflection. But this, that thinking thinks itself and as thinking must think itself, does not in any way sever thinking as a representing from its objects; rather with this it first achieves a mediation and adequate unification with these objects. The dialectical process of thinking is thus no mere succession of representations in human consciousness that can be psychologically observed. The dialectical process is the basic movement in the objectivity of all objects as a whole, i.e., in being in the modern sense. The incident whereby our Western-European thinking has achieved the dimension of dialectic prefigured for it since Plato is a world-historical one. It comes to the humans of this age everywhere and in various forms as the present.

But now what significance does the incident mentioned above have for the task that should concern us here: for the consideration of the laws of thinking? In the brief summary just offered, the answer runs: with thinking's entry into the dimension of dialectic the possibility is opened for the shifting of the laws of thought into the domain of a more fundamental rule. In the horizon of dialectic, the fundamental principles of thinking attain a transformed form. Hegel shows that the laws of thought previously mentioned posit more than and something other than what the common conception immediately finds in their formulations. To be sure, the common conception finds nothing therein. Thus the formula for the law of identity, $A = A$, is taken by the common understanding as a statement that says nothing. Hegel however shows that this statement, A is A, could not even posit what it posits if it had not already breached the empty sameness of A with itself and set A, at the very least, against itself, against A. The proposition could not even be a proposition, i.e., something invariably compound, if it had not first abandoned what it appears to posit, namely A as completely empty sameness, and thus as a sameness of something with itself that is never capable of further unfolding, i.e. A as identity and indeed abstract identity. Consequently Hegel can say, "In the *form of the proposition,* therefore, in which identity is expressed, there lies *more* than simple, abstract identity."[1]

But Hegel in his *Logic* has not only made visible the richer truth of the laws of thought, now brought back to their ground, he has also demonstrated at the same time in an irrefutable manner that our customary thinking, precisely where it proffers itself as correct, does not itself obey the laws of thought at all, but instead constantly contradicts them. This proves to be so, however, only as a consequence of the state of affairs whereby all that is has contradiction at its base, which Hegel asserts often and in multiple ways. Once in the statement "contradiction is the root of all movement and vitality; it is only in so far as something has a contradiction within it that it moves, has an urge and activity."[2] Better known, because catchier and thus often cited, is Hegel's thought concerning the relationship between life and death. The latter, death, is commonly held to be the annihilation and devastation of life. Death stands in contradiction to life. The contradiction tears life and death apart, the contradiction is the tearing [*Zerrissenheit*] of the two. Hegel says, however (in the preface to the *Phenomenology of Spirit*): "But the life of Spirit is not the life that shrinks from death and keeps itself untouched by devastation, but rather the life that endures it and maintains itself in it. It <spirit> wins its truth only when, in utter dismemberment [*Zerrissenheit*] <i.e., in contradiction>, it finds itself."[3] And Hölderlin's late poem "In lovely

1. G. W. F. Hegel, *Wissenschaft der Logik, Zweiter Teil,* ed. Georg Lasson (Leipzig: Felix Meiner Verlag, 1923), 31. G. W. F. Hegel, *Wissenschaft der Logik. Erster Band. Die objective Logik (1812/1813), Gesammelte Werke* vol. 11, ed. Friedrich Hogemann and Walter Jaeschke (Hamburg: Felix Meiner Verlag, 1978), 264. English translation: G. W. F. Hegel, *Hegel's Science of Logic,* trans. A. V. Miller (Atlantic Highlands, N.J.: Humanities Press International, Inc., 1993), 415.

2. Hegel, *Wissenschaft der Logik,* 58. Hegel, *Wissenschaft der Logik, Gesammelte Werke* 11, 286. English translation: Hegel, *Hegel's Science of Logic,* 439.

3. G. W. F. Hegel, *Phänomenologie des Geistes,* ed. Johannes Hoffmeister, 4th ed. (Leipzig: Felix Meiner Verlag, 1937), 29–30. G. W. F. Hegel, *Phänomenologie des Geistes, Gesammelte Werke* vol. 9, ed. Wolfgang Bonsiepen and Reinhard Heede (Hamburg: Felix Meiner Verlag, 1980), 27. English translation: G. W. F. Hegel, *Hegel's Phenomenology of Spirit,* trans. A. V. Miller (Oxford: Oxford University Press, 1977), 19.

blueness blossoms . . ." concludes with the words "Life is death, and death is also a life."[4] Here contradiction is unveiled as what unites and endures. This appears to contradict what Novalis writes in one of his fragments: "to annihilate the principle of contradiction is perhaps the highest task of a higher logic."[5] But the thoughtful poet means to say: The principle of common logic, namely the law of avoiding contradiction, must be annihilated and thus precisely validate contradiction as the basic trait of all that is actual. What Novalis says here is exactly the same as what Hegel thinks: annihilate the principle of contradiction in order to save contradiction as the law of the actuality of the actual.

By this reference to Hegel's dialectical interpretation of the laws of thought, whereby they say more than their formulas state and whose prescriptions have never been followed by dialectical thinking, an exciting state of affairs comes to the fore, the adequate knowledge of which—the decisive experience of which—has not yet reached the ears of current thinking. Admittedly, we need not wonder about this. When even Hegel himself in that part of his *Logic* that deals with the laws of thought pronounces them "the most difficult,"[6] how are we

4. Friedrich Hölderlin, "In lieblicher Bläue . . . ," in *Sämtliche Werke*, historisch-kritische Ausgabe, vol. 6: *1806–1843: Dichtungen, Jugendarbeiten, Dokumente*, ed. Ludwig von Pigenot and Friedrich Seebass, 2nd ed. (Berlin: Propyläen Verlag, 1923), 24–27, 27. English translation: Friedrich Hölderlin, "In Lovely Blueness . . . ," in *Poems & Fragments*, ed. and trans. Michael Hamburger, 3rd ed. (London: Anvil Press Poetry, 1994), 714–19, 719, translation modified.
5. Novalis, Fragment 1125 in *Die Enzyklopädie*, II. Abteilung: Philosophie, 2. "Über die Logik," in Novalis, *Briefe und Werke*, vol. 3, ed. Ewald Wasmuth (Berlin: Lambert Schneider Verlag, 1943), 325–30, 330. Novalis, Entry 101 in "Aufzeichnungen von Juni bis Dezember 1799," in Novalis, *Schriften: Die Werke Friedrich von Hardenbergs*, vol. 3: *Das philosophische Werke II*, ed. Richard Samuel with Hans-Joachim Mähl and Gerhard Schulz (Stuttgart: W. Kohlhammer Verlag, 1968), 556–94, 570.
6. G. W. F. Hegel, *Encyclopädie der Wissenschaften im Grundrisse*, 2nd ed., ed. Georg Lasson (Leipzig: Felix Meiner Verlag, 1911), §114, 128. G. W. F. Hegel, *Enzyklopädie der philosophischen Wissenschaften im Grundrisse (1830)*, *Gesammelte Werke* vol. 20, ed. Wolfgang Bonsiepen and Hans Christian Lucas with assistance from Udo Rameil (Hamburg: Felix Meiner Verlag, 1992), 145. English translation: G. W. F. Hegel, *The Encyclopaedia Logic,*

supposed to find our way without any preparation into that
dimension in which the laws of thought and their founding
become questionable through dialectic?

To be sure, as soon as the talk is of dialectic someone will
bring up dialectical materialism. One takes it for a worldview,
passes it off as an ideology. Indeed, by this assessment we side-
step further contemplation instead of acknowledging: The dialectic is today a, perhaps even the, world reality. Hegel's dialectic is one of those thoughts that—struck up from afar—"direct
the world," equipotent there where dialectical materialism is
revered as there where—in only a slightly modified style of the
same thinking—it is refuted. Behind this confrontation of
worldviews, as one calls it, the struggle for mastery of the earth
rages on. Behind this struggle, however, there reigns a conflict
in which Western thinking itself is entangled with itself. It begins to unfurl itself into its ultimate triumph, which consists in
the fact that this thinking has compelled nature into relin-
quishing atomic energy.

Is it still irrelevant or even immaterial if we think about . . .
thought and attempt a meditation upon its principles? Perhaps in
so doing we arrive at thought on its own ground. Perhaps we
only come across its trail in that we opportunely still detect the
violence of thought, which surpasses every possible quantum of
atomic energy and does so infinitely, i.e., in accordance with its
essence. For nature would never be able to appear as a standing
reserve of energy, as it now is represented, if atomic energy were
not challenged forth along with it by thought, i.e., was put in
place [ge-stellt] by thought. Atomic energy is the object of a com-
putation and steering performed by a scientific technology that
calls itself nuclear physics. That physics reaches this point of positioning nature in this way, however, is a meta-physical incident—if not something else besides.

But if it now were to come to the point that the thinking
being [Wesen] is extinguished by atomic energy, where would
thinking then remain? What is more powerful, natural
energy in its technological-mechanical form or thought? Or
do neither of the two, which in this case belong together, have

trans. T. F. Geraets, W. A. Suchting, and H. S. Harris (Indianapolis, Ind.:
Hackett Publishing Company, 1991), 179.

the privilege? Is there still anything at all when all mortal essencing of the human on earth "is" extinguished?

The thought that thinking followed in pursuing nature into atomic energy is already more dominant [*waltender*] than the power of natural energy, as well as any other thinking of nature, and it has been so from the outset. Such thoughts are not first fabricated by our mortal thinking; rather the latter is constantly only claimed by a thought, either to correspond to it or to renounce it. It is not we, the humans, who come upon these thoughts; the thoughts come to us mortals whose essence is set upon thinking as its ground. But who thinks these thoughts that visit us?—we directly ask, under the assumption that it would be right to ask this question since it immediately imposes itself upon us. Us—who are we who so immediately propose ourselves? How will we even enter into such thoughts, without being experienced in the basic principles of thinking?

"Basic Principles of Thinking"—we begin with an elucidation of the title of the lectures. Through the elucidation a path can open for the following course of thought. The elucidation [*Die Erläuterung*] seeks the limpid [*das Lautere*]. We name air, water, limpid insofar as they are not murky and thus transparent. But there is also genuine [*lauteres*] gold, which remains thoroughly nontransparent. The limpid is the unclouded in the sense that every admixture of what does not belong therein falls away. We are refining [*läutern*] the title "Basic Principles of Thinking" in order to keep away what does not belong. It happens in that we arrive at those determinations that the title would name as the title of the following lectures. The elucidation of the title thus brings us on the path of a thinking that thinks after thinking. "Basic Principles of Thinking" at first means laws for thinking. The latter stands with all of its judgments, concepts, and conclusions under the laws and is ruled by these. Thinking is the object affected by the basic principles. The genitive in the phrasing of the title "Basic Principles of Thinking" means basic principles for thinking. It is a *genitivus obiectivus*.

However, at the same time a second thing shows itself. Principles of the sort A = A, A ≠ not A, are the basic forms of thinking, the principles by which it brings itself into a form. The basic principles thereby prove to be the object that is posited by thinking. This itself is now manifest as the subject of the positing of the basic principles. Kant, after the manner of Descartes, had made visible in the *Critique of Pure Reason* that and how all thinking is essentially an "*I* think. . . ."[7] Everything represented in all thinking, as such, is related back to an "I-think," more precisely stated, everything represented is suffused with this relation to the I-think. If this very relation back upon the same I that thinks did not thoroughly hold sway in our thinking, then we would never be able to think anything. For all thinking, the I in "I think" must be at one with itself and the same as itself.

Fichte has brought this state of affairs into the form "I = I." As distinct from the form for the principle of identity A = A, which formally holds for anything representable whatsoever, the principle "I = I" is determined by a content, similar to the statement we could make of every single tree, for example "tree = tree." But now Fichte shows in his *Wissenschaftslehre* of 1794 that the statement "the tree is the tree" can by no means be set at equal rank with the statement "I am I." Naturally not, we will say, for a tree and my "I" are something different by content. However, all statements of this form, tree = tree, point = point, I = I, fall under the formally empty and thus most universal principle A = A. Yet precisely this is inadmissible according to Fichte. Much more, the statement "I am I" is the expression for that deed of the I, i.e., of the subject, by which the principle A = A is first posited. The principle I = I is more encompassing than the formal universal principle A = A—an exciting state of affairs about which we by no means say too much when we proclaim that what this rests upon has not yet been made clear, which invariably means for thinking that it has not been brought into its inceptual questionability.

At first, thinking is not the object for the basic principles, but rather their subject. The genitive in the title "Basic Principles of Thinking" is a *genitivus subiectivus*. But the basic principles are such also for thinking, they concern it. The genitive in the title

---

7. Translator's Note: See Immanuel Kant, *Kritik der reinen Vernunft*, 2. Auflage 1787, vol. 3 of *Kants gesammelte Schriften*, ed. Königlich Preußischen Akademie der Wissenschaften (Berlin: Georg Reimer, 1911), B 132. English translation: Immanuel Kant, *Critique of Pure Reason*, trans. Paul Guyer and Allen W. Wood (Cambridge: Cambridge University Press, 1999), 246.

is also a *genitivus obiectivus*. Therefore we carefully say: The title "Basic Principles of Thinking" announces something of a double meaning. Thus it poses for us the following interconnected questions: Can and must we bring the title to a univocity and accordingly interpret it only as either *genitivus obiectivus* or *genitivus subiectivus*? Or must we let go of this "either-or" and instead of this let a "both-and" hold sway? The "both-and" is an eagerly sought-out retreat for thinking, especially when it is counting on an unquestioning avoidance of the issue.

The mere "both-and," however, is only a pretense to ward off further thinking. But where it is a matter of contemplating thinking and its basic principles, the "both-and" cannot be an answer, rather only a lead-in to the question: how do things stand with thinking itself if it is supposed to be the subject of its basic principles as much as their object?

"Basic Principles of Thinking"—even a rough elucidation of this title produces a disquiet that we do not wish again to allay. That this may rouse our pondering, we proceed once more in a modified way down the previous path of thought. We ask: does the principle of identity in the form A = A hold because thinking as the "I think . . ." posits it, or must thinking posit this proposition because A = A is the case? What does "is" mean here? Do the basic principles of thinking stem from thinking? Or does thinking stem from what its basic principles posit? What does "posit" mean here? We say, for example, "supposing the case that" and mean assuming that something holds as such and such. But the positing of basic principles is obviously no mere assumption. The basic principles establish something and indeed do so in advance and for all cases. They are consequently presuppositions. To be sure, but even with this word we proceed very liberally and carelessly, without considering who or what here "posits" and in what way, and where "in advance" the posited is thus posited. As laws of thinking, however, the basic principles of thinking posit what they posit as irrevocably fixed. They form the stronghold, as it were, wherein thinking secures all of its undertakings from the outset. Or are the basic principles of thinking—let us recall what Hegel has said of them—no mighty fortress for thinking? For their part, do the basic principles require a concealment and sheltering? But where are they sheltered? Where do they come from? What is the place of origin for the basic principles of thinking? Anyone who would proclaim today that this question has been unanimously decided would be a swindler. He proffers something as science that is not science, that can never be such, because no science reaches that point where the place of origin for the basic principles of thinking could perhaps be discussed. Let us calmly admit it: the provenance of the basic principles of thinking, the place of the thinking that posits these propositions, the essence of the place named here and of its location, all of this remains veiled in the dark for us. This darkness is perhaps in play for all thinking at all times. Humans cannot set it aside. Rather they must learn to acknowledge the dark as something unavoidable and to keep at bay those prejudices that would destroy the lofty reign of the dark. Thus the dark remains distinct from the pitch-black as the mere and utter absence of light. The dark however is the secret of the light. The dark keeps the light to itself. The latter belongs to the former. Thus the dark has its own limpidity. Hölderlin, who truly knew the old wisdom, says in the third strophe of his poem "Remembrance":

> But extend to me,
> full of dark light,
> the fragrant cup[8]

The light is no longer an illuminated clearing, when the light diffuses into a mere brightness, "brighter than a thousand suns."[9] It remains difficult to guard the limpidity of thinking,

---

8. Friedrich Hölderlin, "Andenken," in *Sämtliche Werke*, historisch-kritische Ausgabe, vol. 4: *Gedichte 1800–1806*, ed. Norbert von Hellingrath, 2nd ed. (Berlin: Propyläen Verlag, 1923), 61–63, 61. English translation: Friedrich Hölderlin, "Remembrance," in *Poems & Fragments*, ed. and trans. Michael Hamburger, 3rd ed. (London: Anvil Press Poetry, 1994), 508–11, 509, translation modified.

9. Translator's Note: a citation from *The Bhagavad Gita* (ed. and trans. Laurie L. Patton [New York: Penguin, 2008]), 11.12. The line likewise forms the title of Robert Jungk's 1956 book, *Heller als tausend Sonnen: Das Schicksal der Atomforscher* (Stuttgart: Scherz & Goverts Verlag, 1956), English translation: Robert Jungk, *Brighter than a Thousand Suns: A Personal History of the Atomic Scientists*, trans. James Cleugh (London: Victor Gollancz Ltd., 1958), the first published account of the Manhattan project where Robert Oppenheimer famously recalled these words upon the

i.e., to keep at bay the admixture of the brightness that does not belong and to find the brightness that is alone fitting to the dark. Lao Tzu says, "Whoever knows its brightness, cloaks himself in its darkness."[10] We add to this the truth that everyone knows, but few realize: Mortal thinking must let itself down into the dark depths of the well if it is to see the stars by day. It remains more difficult to guard the limpidity of the dark than to procure a brightness that only wants to shine as such. What wants only to shine, does not illuminate. The textbook presentation of the doctrine of the laws of thought nevertheless needs to appear as though the content of these laws and their absolute validity were immediately illuminating for everyone.

Yet even the first elucidation of the title "Basic Principles of Thinking" led us instantly into the dark. Where the basic principles stem from—whether from thinking itself or from that which thinking at base has to consider, or whether even from neither of these two sources instantly offering themselves—this is concealed from us. Beyond this, through Hegel's dialectical interpretation of thinking, the laws of thought have been demoted from their previously valorized form and role. The entrance of thinking into the dimension of dialectic, however, prohibits us above all from henceforth speaking so easily of thinking "as such" ["dem" Denken]. Thinking "as such," without further ado, is nowhere to be found. If we represent thinking as a universal human capacity then it becomes an imaginary construction. However, if we call upon the fact that in our age everywhere upon the earth a uniform manner of thinking achieves world-historical dominance, then we must just as decisively hold in view that this uniform thinking

---

detonation of the first atomic bomb (see *Heller,* 206; *Brighter,* 198). Heidegger discusses an earlier work of Jungk's in the preparatory studies for his 1953 lecture "The Question Concerning Technology," in Martin Heidegger, *Leitgedanken zur Entstehung der Metaphysik, der neuzeitlichen Wissenschaft und der modernen Technik, Gesamtausgabe* vol. 76, ed. Claudius Strube (Frankfurt am Main: Vittorio Klostermann, 2009), 347.

10. Chapter 28 of Laò-Tsè, *Laò-Tsè's Taò Te King,* trans. Victor von Strauss (Leipzig: Verlag der "Asia Major," 1924), 140. English translation: "Who knows how white attracts, / Yet always keeps himself within black's shade," in Lao Tzu, *The Tao Te Ching,* in *The Texts of Taoism,* ed. F. Max Müller, trans. James Legge (New York: Dover Publications, 1962), 45–124, 71.

is only the form, leveled down and rendered useful, of that historical formation of thought that we name the Western-European, the dispensational singularity of which we scarcely even experience and seldom enough acknowledge.

In an early text published from his manuscript remains, Karl Marx explains that "the entire so-called world history is nothing other than the production of humans by human labor, nothing other than the becoming nature of the human."[11] Many will repudiate this construal of world history and its underlying conception of the essence of the human. But no one can deny that today technology, industry, and economy authoritatively determine all actuality of the actual to be the labor of the self-production of the human. Yet with this assessment we already fall out of that dimension of thinking in which Marx's expression just cited concerning world history as "the labor of the self-production of the human" moves about. For the word "labor" here does not mean mere activity and performance. The word speaks in the sense of Hegel's concept of labor, which is thought as the basic trait of the dialectical process, by which the becoming of the actual unfolds and completes its actuality. That Marx, in opposition to Hegel, does not see the essence of actuality in absolute, self-conceiving spirit, but rather in the human producing itself and its means of living, this indeed brings Marx into the most extreme opposition to Hegel, but by this opposition Marx remains within Hegelian metaphysics; for life and the reign of actuality is above all the labor process as dialectic, i.e., as thinking, insofar as what is genuinely productive of every production remains thinking, whether this thinking is taken

---

11. Karl Marx, *Der Historische Materialismus: Die Frühschriften*, ed. Siegfried Landshut and J. P. Mayer, 2 vols. (Stuttgart: Alfred Kröner Verlag, 1932), vol. 1, 307. Karl Marx, *Werke, Artikel, Entwürfe. März 1843 bis August 1844, Marx-Engels Gesamtausgabe* vol. I.2, ed. Institut für Marxismus-Leninismus beim Zentralkomitee der Sozialistischen Einheitspartei Deutschlands (Berlin: Dietz Verlag, 1982), 274. English translation: *Economic and Philosophic Manuscripts of 1844*, trans. Martin Milligan and Dirk J. Struik, in *The Collected Works of Marx and Engels*, vol. 3: *Early Works: 1835–1844*, ed. Maria Shcheglova, Tatyana Grishina, Lyudgarda Zubrilova, Tatyana Butkova, and Larisa Miskievich (New York: International Publishers, 1975), 229–346, 305.

up and accomplished as something speculative-metaphysical or scientific-technological, or a mishmash and oversimplification of the two. Every pro-duction is in itself already re-flection, is thinking.

If we therefore risk what the title implies, to consider thinking *as such*, then the talk of thinking *as such* only has a reliable sense when we experience thinking everywhere and only as that which determines our historical Dasein. As soon as we attempt to fundamentally contemplate this thinking, we find ourselves already introduced to the tensions and relations of our history, which means contemporary world history. Only if we are sufficiently experienced in our thinking, in the essential breadth of it, are we capable of recognizing another thinking as foreign and of listening to it in its productive strangeness as foreign. But the thinking, itself historical, that today determines world history does not stem from today, is older than what is merely past, and wafts to us in its most ancient thoughts from out of a nearness whose trace we do not detect, because we suppose that what concernfully approaches us authentically, i.e., essentially, would be something current.

Lecture II and
Review of Lecture I

No one can demand of us that we should think like the philosophers. But it could be expected of us, from who knows where, that we learn to make distinctions, because differences do flare up and by means of these we return to the simple and enter into it in such a way that the simple, now seen as something astonishing, is never relinquished by us again. We all think in some way or other and yet are all inexperienced with the issue of whether and how the grounding-principles of thinking move or even come to rest.

In the present age, the raging storm of world historical battles for mastery of the earth has at its center the calm of a strife in which Western-European thinking has remained entangled since its beginning. It is the essential strife of thinking with that which calls it to think what it thinks and thus to think how it thinks. The chains by which it would be entangled in this primordial strife are of the sort that Hölderlin once named when he poetically asked, in regard to the relationship between the gods and the mortals:

> Who was it who first
> Defiled the bonds of love
> And turned them into chains?[1]

---

1. Strophe VII of Friedrich Hölderlin, "Der Rhein," in *Sämtliche Werke,* historisch-kritische Ausgabe, vol. 4: *Gedichte 1800–1806,* ed. Norbert von Hellingrath, 2nd ed. (Berlin: Propyläen Verlag, 1923), 172–80, 175. English translation: Friedrich Hölderlin, "The Rhine," in *Poems & Fragments,*

Whenever and however we attempt to contemplate thinking, every time a blunt consideration is already revealed to us: there is no thinking as such [*das Denken*]. Thinking—and the talk can be of this alone—is the hidden and innermost dispute of our history. Thinking is what is historical of this history and thus is historical in itself.

At first the title "Basic Principles of Thinking" proved itself to be equivocal in the sense of a double meaning that the genitive brings with it as *genitivus obiectivus* and *genitivus subiectivus*. Now it becomes clear: The genitive in the title is equivocal, and thus ensnaring, in yet another way entirely.

That thinking whose basic principles would concern us appears to be thinking plain and simple, taken absolutely and universally. In truth, however, this thinking is restricted to the historicality of Western-European history, although, as restricted to this, it is at the same time unleashed as the fundamental characteristic of the modern world technology of our planetary age. When we say thinking "as such," then this can mean thinking as general human activity; however, it can also mean thinking as a singular destiny of Western humanity.

The first equivocality mentioned in the title "Basic Principles of Thinking" was apparently only the grammatical dual meaning of the genitive. The equivocality just mentioned is an ambiguity behind which a world-historical indecisiveness concerning the essence of thinking plays itself out. By no means does this ambiguity merely stand next to that dual meaning. Rather the one equivocality as well as the other both stem from the same source into which we must inquire. Accordingly, the multiply equivocal title of the lectures, assuming we now hear it contemplatively, is a hint into the question of how we keep to thinking, of whether we are inclined to experience it in terms of the basic principles.

Assuming therefore that thinking in itself would not only be historically determining, but dispensationally determined, then must not every meditation upon a thinking that is in itself historical for its part be in a similar predicament, i.e., be historical? But then does this not say that we first would have

---

ed. and trans. Michael Hamburger, 3rd ed. (London: Anvil Press Poetry, 1994), 430–43, 437, translation modified.

to acquire a comprehensive and penetrating historiological overview of the history of Western thinking before we could hazard to contemplate thinking? No.

Historiological knowledge does not bring us into the history of the thoughts that guide the world. Historiological knowledge represents what was thought earlier as something past, offers evidence for the past, but still attests to no historicality. Even when the representations concerning the past are historiologically-philologically correct, and thus certain within the limits of science, and even if we employ these correct representations concerning the past toward the goal of a comparison with the contemporary, it never gets to the point that an earlier thought concernfully approaches us by lifting us up and out of these historiological conceptions concerning thinking. Up and out to where?

Historiological knowledge concerning what was previously thought—taken on its own and tallied—does not yet guarantee that we send ourselves with our whole essence into that thinking that, from far off beyond us, is given to us in thought by the oldest thoughts of Western thinking, which themselves thereby come upon us. In the meantime, they come. They remain on the way in their arrival, even when we do not attend to them because we are single-mindedly obsessed with analyzing the current situation so as to be able to plan the next one. The industry of continuous analysis of the situation is one thing, but another is the reserved historical glance into the constellation. This is the present that avows to us that and how the most ancient Western thoughts—quietly reigning as on their earliest day—determine and carry out the essence of modern world technology.

Nietzsche says of those thoughts that "guide the world" that they "come on doves' feet."[2] Thus it requires a fine ear to perceive

2. Friedrich Nietzsche, *Also Sprach Zarathustra* (Zweiter Theil, "Die stillste Stunde"), in *Nietzsche' Werke, Großoktavausgabe,* vol. 6 (Leipzig: C. G. Naumann, 1923), 217. Friedrich Nietzsche, *Also Sprach Zarathustra,* kritische Gesamtausgabe, vol. 6.1, ed. Giogrio Colli and Mazzino Montinari (Berlin: Walter de Gruyter, 1989), 185. English translation: *Thus Spoke Zarathustra,* ed. and trans. Walter Kaufmann (New York: Viking Penguin, 1978), 146.

Cf. also Friedrich Nietzsche, *Der Wille zur Macht,* "Vorwort," *Nietzsche' Werke, Großoktavausgabe,* vol. 15, 3rd ed. (Leipzig: C. G. Naumann, 1922), 4.

the coming and the provenance of world-guiding thinking. The historical ear is fine when it is addressed to the appeal. In order to address it in this way, listening must be free, i.e., open, within the breadth of the dispensation that is avowed to the ear. Before all else, such a listening into the provenance of the thoughts that are thought to us must have set aside that form of representation according to which hearing itself is only understood as the act of a subject that draws its objects or, what holds here just as well, other subjects into its sphere. In this schema of the subject-object relation, or even that of the subject-subject, there also belongs the I-thou relation, so strongly emphasized today. Here the standard conceptions remain stuck in the apprehension of the human as a subject, i.e., in Cartesianism.

As long as one pays homage to this conception of the human as a subject or a person, thinking is closed off against the arriving of the dispensation avowed to us. One can then logically proclaim that every speaking with history, since it is indeed arranged by a subject, would only ever be a self-made monologue. This opinion comes to everyone quite naturally because one is accustomed to conceiving the human as a subject. The liberation from this inadequate conception of the human will not be achieved so long as we resort to procuring arguments that this conception would be false. Liberation from this conception requires something simple, that we abandon it in favor of an experience in which we are already residing. In all brevity, this can be stated so: We only catch sight of that which has already sighted us. So that this relationship between sighting and catching sight can purely hold sway, we must abandon the position of the human as a subject, and thereby the subject-object relation, and have found our way back into a more originary dimension of the human essence. We only catch sight of what has already sighted us, and indeed without our knowledge or effort. We only hear that to which we already belong insofar as we stand in its claim. But precisely within this relationship between sighting and claim, on the one hand, and catching sight and hearing on the other, is housed the danger that we mishear in our hearing, that

---

Friedrich Nietzsche, *Der Wille zur Macht* (Stuttgart: Alfred Kröner, 1996), 3. English translation: *The Will to Power*, ed. Walter Kaufmann, trans. Walter Kaufmann and R. J. Hollingdale (New York: Vintage Books, 1968), 3.

we lose sight and overlook in our catching sight, and thus fall prey to something arbitrary.

The relationship to what concernfully approaches us as a sighting and a claim, to what comes upon us, to what is impending [*Gegen-wart*] and thus is authentically destiny and history, this relationship to history remains as simple as today it is difficult for us to even achieve and retain such a relationship. The reason for this difficulty lies not only in the representation of the human as a subject, but also in the representation of history as an object and formation of historiology and of historiological consciousness. Both manners of representation, that of the human as a subject and that of history as historiology, belong together in the same kinship. They are of a modern provenance and reach their most extreme unified development in dialectic. The Middle Ages knew a historiological consciousness in the rigorously construed sense just as little as Antiquity knew the conception of the human as a subject. That one nevertheless without inhibition reads both manners of representation into the Middle Ages and Antiquity, not to mention the corresponding interpretations, has its simple basis in the uninterrupted dominance of historiological and subjective representing. The subject of the historiological conception of history is each time to be found in the most modern self-consciousness of our age.

Faced with the unbroken dominance of subjectivity and historiology it remains a stroke of luck if we perceive throughout the age the soft steps of the world-guiding thoughts, in order to follow them from whither they have come [*ihrer Zukunft*] back into their place of origin [*Herkunft*], so that their arrival [*Ankunft*] would concernfully approach us.

The thinking that now determines world history and is itself more historical than the course of world historiological occurrences, only addresses our contemplation when it delivers us over to its claim. While we say this, a consideration imposes itself that is so immediately illuminating we can no longer keep it aside. We are given the following to consider.

How should a tradition reach us if not through historiology? How is historiology supposed to work securely if not in the methodical form of the historiological-philological sciences? Yet, tradition, i.e., that a claim of what has-been brings itself into the space of freedom and that history thereby speaks to us, such tradition does not rest on the historiological knowledge procured by us, but rather all historiology is each time only a particular kind of technological-practical refinement and presentation of that tradition. All historiology requires history. But history does not necessarily need historiology. Thus there are peoples who know no historiology although they live historically, perhaps even in a deeper sense. Admittedly, we today are still all too accustomed to understand the titles "history" and "historiology" indiscriminately, at one moment objectively, at another epistemologically.

The country that counts among its great thinkers R. Descartes, the founder of the doctrine of the subjectivity of human beings, has no word in its language for history [*Geschichte*] to distinguish it from historiology [*Historie*]. No one of any insight will proclaim that this is by chance. There where a language has to say what is essential for it, there is no chance.

Because we continually throw the words "history" and "historiology" heedlessly together, along with the manners of representation and issues pertaining to them, and are incapable of drawing any essential distinction between them, the opinion can take hold that human races and peoples that know no historiology consequently live unhistorically. Of the same style— only the reverse—is the opinion that repudiating or overcoming the predominance of historiology would also eradicate the historicality of a Dasein, would render history and its tradition essenceless. Against this, and in what follows we will attempt to bring about an experience of this, we say anew: Because it itself is historically attuned [ge-*stimmt*], the thinking which determines [be*stimmt*] contemporary world history only speaks to our contemplation when it has delivered us over to its claim.

Accordingly, our undertaking—to experience thinking from its basic principles—proves itself a historical risk. This remains far removed from the presumption of pronouncing absolutely valid laws "of" thinking. But now it also becomes all too significant that the title "Basic Principles of Thinking" indicates the historical undertaking of these lectures in a richly undetermined manner. At best, the elucidation of the title has perhaps brought us to the path of the lectures, but it has by no means set us out along it. An elucidation of the mere title, even one of this kind, still cannot at all enter into the issue at stake. The provided elucidation remains perforce a precaution for the proceedings, but is not yet the entry into the matter, i.e., the strife, in which Western thinking is inceptually entangled. It would then have to be that the title "Basic Principles of Thinking" speaks a language entirely its own, a language that takes away from it the role of being merely a title and grants it the linguistic character of an address [*An-spruchs*].

For all too long now we have spoken of thinking without having brought along a useful clarification of what this means: thinking.

Even if we admit, whether from insight and voluntarily or against our will and with doubts, that our Western thinking not only *has* a history, but rather itself *is* a, perhaps the, basic characteristic of contemporary world history, then before proceeding any further, and in order to do just this, we may demand a satisfactory account of what one generally understands by thinking. We would even have to demand this, if we are not to tumble about in a fuzzy use of the word "thinking." Admittedly, at the same time we must also keep in view that the current, worn-down conception of thinking lives off of the historical tradition. Thus we must prepare ourselves to set out along the path the tradition has cut and which it keeps to, the path leading from the early days of the history of thinking and directed toward our present.

How are we now supposed to find the path to an adequate characterization of that which, according to the tradition, is thinking? Is there a signpost for this path? Indeed. It stands so inconspicuously and freely before us that we easily pass over it, without exactly reading its directive. (With signposts, anyway, it is a peculiar matter. They certainly provide a directive, but remain away from the path. Instead of going along with us, they leave us to our own devices in going along the path.)

Since long ago and still for the modern dialectic up until our day, meditation upon thinking bears the name "logic." This word "logic" is the signpost. Logic is the name for the knowledge that concerns the λόγος. Logic, however, now counts as the doctrine of thinking. Correspondingly, the basic characteristic of thinking shows itself to us in the λόγος. If a thinking is logical, it keeps to its order. For contemporary thinking, logic has become still more logical, on account of which it has been

given the modified name "logistics." By this name, logic pro-
cures its ultimate—which means universal—and planetary
form of dominance. In the age of technology, this appears in the
form of the machine. The computers that are set to work in
business and industry, in the research institutes of science, and
in the organizational centers of politics, we surely cannot conceive as devices merely employed for more rapid calculation.
The thinking-machine in itself is already much more the consequence of a transposition of thinking into a manner of
thought that, as mere calculation, provokes a translation into
the machinery of these machines. Thus we overlook what happens here as an alteration of thinking, as long as we do not keep
our eyes open to the fact that thinking must become logistical
because it is inceptually logical.

To what extent must thinking be logical? Logical means here:
in accordance with the λόγος. Thinking must be logical because
its essence is determined by the λόγος. The λόγος comes to us in
the affairs and words of the Ancient Greeks. What does the Greek
word λόγος say? Grammatically explained, as a part of speech, it
is the nominalization of the verb λέγειν. This means to gather, to
lay together. In λόγος it is a matter of a gathering as much as of a
laying. Nevertheless, it is necessary that we submit the German
words doing the translating, "gathering" [sammeln] and "laying"
[legen], to the Greek manner of experience so that we can contemplate the words as a translation for λόγος. The Greek word
λέγειν still speaks in the name dialectic; διαλέγεσθαι means to go
through something in laying it together. Such a laying that runs
through everything is called in our language pondering [Überle-
gen]; this means to contemplate something and thus to attest to
the thought. If one will still not notice, then this reference would
like to show anew: According to the pronouncement of our own
language, thinking as pondering [Überlegen], expositing [Darle-
gen], interpreting [Auslegen], attending [Belegen], establishing
[Festlegen], inevitably has to do with Legen [laying] and indeed in
the sense of λέγειν and the λόγος. Yet by this reference to the connection between λόγος, laying, and thinking, we still do not yet
experience the way in which logic interprets [aus-legt] and thus
establishes [fest-legt] λόγος as the basic trait of thinking.

As soon as we inquire about this, the appearance arises that
we have lost ourselves in a historiological report about the past

efforts of the Ancient Greek thinkers to define thinking by λόγος. Yet the λόγος of Ancient thinking is so little antiquated that it remains present just as much in the ancient as in the most modern appearances of world history. What would theology, sociology, physiology, zoology, mineralogy, be without the λόγος? The λόγος speaks throughout all the sciences, whether their name includes the word λόγος or not. The λόγος speaks completely in technology, if we understand by this the whole of the sciences through which technology in the narrower sense is founded. And not only in every sort of science, but through all our representing, calculating, willing, and pursuing, in every sensing and aspiring, the λόγος speaks. More pointedly, though for many ears hard to bear, it must nevertheless be averred: We may travel in electric trains or automobiles, fly in airplanes or sit in movie houses and in front of the television, we may use the refrigerator or the vacuum cleaner, but everywhere we reside in the realm of the λόγος, which logic long ago first sought to comprehend. What comes upon us today as the concealed essence of modern technology, and not the individual technological devices, this essence bears the countenance and the stamp of the λόγος. We still lack the eyes to see the essential countenance of the λόγος, to endure its sighting, and to bring to this the fitting countergaze. In relation to the essential provenance of what is named by the word λόγος, a word of Stefan George's from 1919 that thinks ahead to a later time holds here:

> Hearken to what the somber earth says:
> You free as bird or fish—
> Wherein you hang suspended—that you know not.
> Perhaps a later mouth will find:
> You sat with us at our table
> You lived with us off our fund.
> A beautiful and new vision came to you
> But time grew old. today there is no man alive
> You know not if one will ever come
> Who can still see this vision.[3]

---

3. Stefan George, *Das neue Reich, Gesamt-Ausgabe der Werke, endgültige Fassung*, vol. 9 (Berlin: Georg Bondi, 1928), 129. Translator's Note: the transcription here diverges slightly from the published text.

The λόγος is interpreted by logic as the doctrine of thinking. The essence of thinking rests and resonates in the essence of the λόγος. What does logic teach about the λόγος? The answer would be far too long, were we not to restrict ourselves in the course of these lectures to the determination of the λόγος that has remained directive since Greek Antiquity. It stems from Aristotle, whom one likes to name the father of Western logic, and it follows on the precedent of Plato.

What did Aristotle see in the λόγος when he examined it in a respect that remains standard, in a certain sense, for the subsequent development of logic, but which in its originality cannot be included? What Aristotle saw in the λόγος of logic we take from the adjective that he attached to the λόγος. Aristotle names the λόγος of logic, i.e., the basic trait of thinking: λόγος ἀποφαντικός. This adjective belongs to the verb ἀποφαίνεσθαι, which means to bring something from itself to appear here at the fore. As ἀποφαντικός, the λόγος is the gathering that lays before such that it is able to bring something to the fore. The λόγος brings to the fore that which up until now and each time does not properly appear, though it already lies before us.

Let us take an example. A λόγος of the kind that Aristotle has in view, we invoke when we say, "The path is long." Let us attend now to this λόγος, "The path is long," in the inconspicuous form in which we quietly think of it along a hike. This λόγος is ἀποφαντικός insofar as it brings the long path to the fore for us, gathers it before us, lets it lie before us. And suddenly we note that the elucidation of thinking, i.e., of the λόγος and of λέγειν as a laying, is really not as bewildering and irrelevant as it might first appear.

Thought in a Greek manner, "laying" means letting something lie before, namely what is already lying before, what is presencing, such that it shows itself thereby as what is lying before. The adjective ἀποφαντικός, enabling the letting appear of something, namely from itself and to here, is nothing less than the fitting interpretation of what the λόγος of logic accomplishes as a gathering laying: a letting lie before. Thus Aristotle can concisely name this λόγος, i.e., the basic act of thinking, ἀποφαντικός. This word can hardly be translated; verbosely and less beautifully we would have to say: letting what presences from itself appear here. We translate λόγος ἀποφαντικός more fittingly and with one word: exposition [*Darlegung*], whereby with exposing [*Dar-legen*, lit. laying-there] we hear the Greek sense of λέγειν: letting what appears lie before.

It is enough if we now realize: the λόγος of logic—and therefore thinking—is for the Greeks a letting appear. The Ancient Greeks think with their eyes, i.e., through glances. The λόγος, thinking, is a letting appear of what here has come to appearance from itself, of what is brought into the light from out of the darkness and its sheltering. With this, thinking thus becomes a true thinking, a letting appear that each time in a certain respect discloses and lights up what is concealed. Hereby what is dark is not dissolved in a vain brightness, but rather the dark remains what is concealed and thereby itself first comes to appearance. The light remains invariably a dark light.[4]

The basic action of the λόγος is the letting appear of what lies before. This λόγος is the basic act of thinking. If we experience thinking in its logical essence in terms of the λόγος, then it is revealed: Thinking dwells inceptually in the essential space of a dark light. This is the location where the gods were present to the Greeks.

In this location, we must retrieve what thinking was for the Greeks, λόγος ἀποφαντικός: the unconcealing exposition of what presences.

Meanwhile, one was obliged to represent the λόγος of logic, the main characteristic of thinking, as a proposition. The cited λόγος, "The path is long," can serve as the model of a simple proposition. It falls in the company of propositions like the circle is round, the chalk is white, the house is large, propositions that wander like ghosts through the textbooks of logic and grammar as lifeless models. The statement quietly thought while on a hike, "The path is long," taken as an example of the usual doctrine of the proposition, falls out of its realm so that we are no longer able to catch sight of its corporeal, living statement-character. Thus we must now elucidate—again in the most concise way—what the word "proposition" [*Satz*] means, if we use it appropriately as a translation for the λόγος of logic and want to duly understand the talk of grounding-principles [*den Grund-Sätzen*].

---

4. Truth—ἀλήθεια—the disclosure of what is concealed, and that means at the same time the preservation of it.

Statement means in our older language setting together, composition—as still in music, the movement [*Satz*] of a sonata. In light of this determination that understands the statement as a setting together, we observe the cited example of a λόγος: The path is long. Here we obviously and quite easily come across a setting together. We know it from school. The simple statement sets a sentence subject, namely the path, together with its predicate, namely "long." The path is long. The word for the setting together, for the binding of subject and predicate, we find in the "is," a word that is thus called the copula. If we hold exclusively to this interpretation of the statement, already delineated at the beginning of logic, we never again find our way back to the original statement-character that is appropriate to the λόγος as the disclosive exposition of what lies before.

The Greek word for statement reads σύνθεσις, θέσις. Indeed everything depends on thinking θέσις in a Greek manner, precisely as positing, positioning in the sense of setting up, bringing to a stand, letting stand, namely of that which presences, just as it stands. In the Greek understanding of θέσις, the sense of letting-lie-before resonates. Thus the word θέσις positing—for us something entirely bewildering—can in Greek mean so much as situation [*Lage*]—that which lies before.

If we note that, thought in a Greek manner, positing and proposition say the same as letting lie before, then a view into the genuine statement-character of λόγος opens up for us. According to this, the statement is not originarily the setting together of subject and predicate, but instead, spoken in terms of the example, the letting lie before of the long path that lies before. So the long path—appearing through the ἀπόφανσις—is brought together with us, and we think it in the manner of λόγος as ἀπόφανσις: The long path is, as such, gathered up to us. The genuine statement—the originary setting together—is this gathering to ourselves of the long path that lies before, the gathering of this bringing together of the path with ourselves. The genuine subject—literally that which already lies before—for said statement is not the path or even the concept of the path, but rather the presencing long path itself. This lies at the basis of the whole statement "The path is long." The simple statement accordingly lets lie before that which lies at the basis of its positing. That which lies before and at the basis of the statement is its ground. What is proven [*be-legt*] from this ground is what the simple λόγος exposes [*dar-legt*]. This proving from a ground is a founding. Thus every statement of this kind would be, rigorously thought, a grounding-principle [*Grund-Satz*].

The λόγος of logic, the main characteristic of thinking, as a disclosive exposition is a grounding of the ground [*Ergründen des Grundes*] and thus a founding [*Begründen*] of the statement. It has long been held self-evident that someone who thinks and brings forth thoughts also founds these thoughts. We think nothing of it, that this should be so. But now it becomes clear: Because thinking as λόγος is the exposition of what lies at the ground, founding belongs to thinking not merely as a necessary accompaniment, but from the very outset. It is then revealed: Every λόγος of logic is, as a statement, a grounding-principle in the broadest sense as elucidated here; it lets lie before what already lies before and lies at the ground and thereby brings this to an appearing.

If now every simple statement as statement—as the disclosive exposition of what lies at ground—is already a statement that each time goes to a ground and thus in the broadest sense is a grounding-principle, then what is the essence of those principles known by the title "laws of thought"? What are these laying at the ground and which ground is it that the grounding-principles, properly so called, expose? Obviously nothing that lies before and lies at the ground like the long path, the high mountain, the wide river, the clear night, the cheerful child, the distant god—not any of these, but rather?

We perceive the answer to the question at which we have now arrived just as soon as we attend to the formal nature of the previously introduced basic principles of thinking. The principle of identity reads: A is A. The statement has the form of a λόγος. What does the statement expose? What does it bring to appearance of all that lies before? Not this or that particular thing? Therefore something general? Therefore any arbitrary indeterminate entity that lies before? By no means. The statement A is A exposes A as A. The statement is so little swept away into an indefinite emptiness that it binds itself in a singular determination. A is A. Toward what is the exposition directed? Toward that which belongs to everything that lies before: [that it is the] same as itself. More precisely spoken: This sameness does not belong to everything that lies before like some general condition. Rather, everything that lies before belongs in a sameness with itself, for otherwise something that lies before could never lie before us of itself.

The sameness with itself of what lies before, identity so understood, does not lie next to what lies before, each time in addition to it. Identity is itself nothing that lies before, but it co-constitutes what lies before as such. What appears to lie at the ground of the basic principle A is A, this ground that the statement exposes, the sameness of something with itself, is nothing that lies before, nothing that lies at ground, and in this sense it is no longer ground. But because it is no longer a ground, we speak in a rigorous and sober sense of an abyss [Ab-grund]. The statements that are called basic principles of thinking in an exceptional sense lead us—when we adequately think them—to the abyss. An abyss, however, can no longer be exposed, when exposition means to bring to appearance what lies before and at the ground as ground. How then can we still think statements that lead thinking to its abyss? Thinking only reaches into its abyss when it sets itself apart from every ground. In such setting apart the kind of setting and kind of statement have already altered. Principle now no longer means θέσις, rather *saltus*. The principle becomes a leap. Grounding-principles are leaps that set themselves apart from every ground and leap into the abyss of thinking. In the word "grounding-principle" as now elucidated there necessarily appears something absurd. Grounding-principles, i.e., leaps into the abyss of thinking. Yet the absurdity that surfaces here for a moment is neither invented and artificial, nor is it nonsense. Something else arises: The elucidation of the title "Basic Principles of Thinking" now first achieves its goal. It takes away from the title its role as a mere title.

Basic principles of thinking—this now speaks as a claim upon the leaps of thinking into its abyss. Whether the basic principles of thinking as first named, the cited laws of thought, for their part are already such leaps into the abyss remains open. In any case, Hegel's interpretation of the laws of thought that was touched upon in the first lecture precludes that they become leaps into the abyss of thinking.

Grounding-leaps of thinking—The title now betrays its precision. Namely, the definite article "the" basic principles is not left off because only a few of the laws of thought are to be treated instead of all of them, but rather because the ostensive title prompts us to risk still-inexperiencable and vast leaps of thinking into its abyss. The basic principles of thinking, commonly so called, could presumably be an impetus for that. (The next lecture, which will be held during the week of the university anniversary on Thursday the 27th of June in the town hall, titled "The Principle of Identity," takes the principle here mentioned as the occasion for an attempt to at least prepare for a leap of thinking into its abyss.)

Now the talk of a leap into the abyss instantly awakens the impression as if it concerned a particular deep and ghoulish or even destructive plan. Yet the talk of a leap into the abyss intends an affair that entirely alters the sense for us, but without forcing us into a murky fuzziness. What is meant by leap is the transformation of the thinking that determines our age world-historically. If such a transformation can ever occur at all, then it needs for this a leap that departs from the thinking that has become calculation. Now a leap indeed begins with a departure, yet how the leap will leap and to where it will leap is already determined in advance by the leap and solely by it. Whether and how far humans may succeed in such a leap of thinking is not up to them. On the contrary, it behooves us to prepare for the leap. This consists in guiding our thinking to the leap of departure. This is a thoroughly sober affair. The sober counts for us as the dry, if not even the bland. Sober [*Nüchtern*] comes from *nocturnus*, nocturnal. The preparation of the grounding-leaps of thinking, i.e., of the leaps of thinking into its abyss, is a matter of a kind of nocturne. According to what has been said, this will be an abyss for thinking only of such a sort that thinking as something transformed finds in this abyss a fitting realm for itself. This abyss, however, is nearer to us mortals than we might like to suppose.

Hölderlin sings in one of the late hymns:

> For they are not capable
> of everything, the heavenly ones. Namely,
> the mortals reach sooner into the abyss . . .[5]

---

5. Friedrich Hölderlin, *"Mnemosyne, erste Fassung,"* in *Sämtliche Werke, Stuttgarter Hölderlin Ausgabe*, vol. 2:1, *Gedichte Nach 1800*, ed. Friedrich

Let us note it well: it is the mortals who reach sooner into the abyss, therefore they are the ones who dwell in the refuge of death and are thus able to die. An animal cannot die; it comes to an end. This may go along with the fact that the animal cannot think. Thinking lives by an elective affinity with death.

We see ourselves brought before a distinction:

Basic principles of thinking in the sense of those laws of thought concerning which Hegel has shown that no thinking follows them—and—grounding-leaps of thinking in the sense of a leap of thinking into its abyss.

And yet, the abyss of thinking is not equivalent to the abyss that the poet names.

Beissner (Stuttgart: W. Kohlhammer Verlag, 1951), 193–94, 193. Translator's Note: For an English translation of the second version of "Mnemosyne" featuring these same lines, see Friedrich Hölderlin, "Mnemosyne," in *Hymns and Fragments*, ed. and trans. Richard Sieburth (Princeton, N.J.: Princeton University Press, 1984), 116–19, 117, translation modified.

Lecture III,
The Principle of Identity

According to a customary formulation, the principle of identity reads: A = A. The principle holds as the highest law of thought. We will attempt to contemplate this principle for awhile. We hear the principle as an expression about identity. By means of this principle we would like to find out what identity means.

When thinking is addressed by an issue and then goes after this, it can happen that it changes along the way. Thus it is advisable in what follows to attend more to the *path* and less to the content. To duly linger upon the content would already block the progress of the lecture for us.

What does the formula A = A, which one is obliged to present as the principle of identity, say? The formula names the equivalence of A and A. To an equating there belong at least two. One A is equal to another. Does the principle of identity claim to express such a thing? Apparently not. The identical, Latin *idem*, is called in Greek τὸ αὐτό. Translated into our German language, τὸ αὐτό means "the same." When one continually says the same—for instance, the plant is a plant—he speaks in a tautology. For something to be able to be the same, one is enough. Two are not required for this as they are for equivalence.

The formula A = A speaks of equivalence. It does not name A as the same. The customary formulation of the principle of identity thereby conceals precisely what the principle is trying to say: A is A, i.e., every A is the same as itself.

While we circumscribe the identical in this way, there resounds an old word by which Plato makes the identical perceptible, a word that points back to one still older. In the dialogue *Sophist* 254d, Plato speaks of στάσις and κίνησις, of standstill and transformation. Plato has the stranger say here: Οὐκοῦν αὐτῶν ἕκαστον τοῖν μὲν δυοῖν ἕτερόν ἐστιν, αὐτὸ δ' ἑαυτῷ ταὐτόν.[1] "Now it is indeed the case for you that each of the two is another, but itself the same as itself." Plato says not merely ἕκαστον αὐτὸ ταὐτόν "each itself the same" but αὐτὸ ἑαυτῷ ταὐτόν, "each itself *to itself* the same." The dative signifies: Each something is itself given back to itself, every self is the same— namely *for* it itself, *with* it itself. Here the Greek language evinces a preference for explaining the identical by the same word and through a combination of its various permutations, just as our German language does.

Accordingly, the more fitting formulation for the principle of identity, A is A, says not only every A is itself the same, but rather every A is itself with itself the same. For the sameness of the same, each time only one is required, but in the sameness of the one itself, however, a relationship appears: Each one itself is the same *with* it itself. In sameness there lies this relationship of the *with*, thus a mediation, a binding, a synthesis, a unification in unity. Thus it comes about that throughout the history of Western thinking identity appears with the character of a unity. This unity, however, is by no means the bland emptiness of a relationless monotony. But for this relationship within the same to finally come to the fore—the relationship reigning in identity, already resounding from early on, decided and cast *as* a mediation within itself—indeed, for even an accommodation to be found for this shining forth of mediation within identity, Western thinking required more than two thousand years. The philosophy of speculative idealism in Fichte, Schelling, and Hegel, as prepared for by Kant, was the first to accommodate the essence of identity as in itself synthetic. This cannot be shown here. Only one thing is to be retained: Since the epoch of speculative idealism, it remains forbidden for thinking to conceive the unity of identity in a

---

1. Plato, *Platonis Opera*, vol. 1, ed. John Burnet (Oxford: Oxford University Press, 1899), 254d14–15. English translation: *Sophist*, trans. Nicholas P. White, in *Plato: Complete Works*, ed. John M. Cooper and D. S. Hutchinson (Indianapolis, Ind.: Hackett Publishing Company, 1997), 235–93, 277.

merely empty manner as sheer monotony and to disregard the synthesis and mediation reigning in this unity.

Even in the improved formulation, A is A, only an abstract identity comes to the fore. Henceforth this much is clear: The principle of identity tells us nothing about identity. Presumably it does not even claim to tell us such. It is held to be the highest law of thought. As law [*Ge-setz*]—we hear this word like our word "mountain range" [*Gebirg*]—as law, the principle of identity gathers all the positing of all the statements [*alles Setzen aller Sätze*] in an authoritative way. Which way?

We hear the standard when we attend to the tonic pitch [*Grundton*] of the principle of identity and accordingly emphasize its formulation: No longer merely A is A, but rather A *is* A. Now what do we hear?

The principle speaks of the "is," of how every being is, namely, it itself the same with itself. The principle of identity speaks of the *being* of beings. As a law of thinking, the principle only holds insofar as it is a law of being, this says: For every being as such there belongs identity, the unity with itself.

Heard in its tonic pitch, what the principle of identity expresses is precisely what the entirety of Western-European thought thinks, namely: The unity of identity forms a basic characteristic of the being of beings. Accordingly, all of our comporting to beings of every kind stands under the claim of identity. Were this claim not to speak, then the being could never appear in its being. Consequently, there would also be no science. Were the sameness of its object not guaranteed in advance, science could not be what it is. Research everywhere lays claim to this guarantee. All the same, the leading conception of identity never brings any conceivable use to the sciences. But the claim of the identity of the object has always already spoken in the sciences, both before and during the attempts at producing fruitful conceptions and types of procedures. (From their first step to their last, the sciences must correspond to the claim of the identity of objects, regardless of whether they properly hear this claim or not.)

The claim of identity speaks from the being of beings. According to the teachings of philosophy, identity is a basic characteristic of being. But now in Western thinking at its earliest, where the being of beings properly speaks, namely in Parmenides, τὸ αὐτό, the identical, speaks not only in the sense mentioned, but in still another almost excessive sense. One of the fragments reads: τὸ γὰρ αὐτὸ νοεῖν ἐστίν τε καὶ εἶναι.[2] "The same, namely, is perceiving (thinking) as well as also being."

Here what are different, namely thinking and being, are referred to the same. What does this say? Something entirely different from what we know as the basic doctrine of Western thinking, that identity belongs to being. Against this, the cited statement of Parmenides says: Being belongs with thinking in the same. Would being consequently be a characteristic of identity?

Indeed what then does identity mean here? What does the word τὸ αὐτό, the same, say in the fragment of Parmenides? Parmenides gives no answer. Here we do not find out how we are to think τὸ αὐτό, the same.

Where identity itself speaks, and not merely the principle of identity, its pronouncement stipulates that thinking and being belong together in the same. But now we have unintentionally already given a meaning to τὸ αὐτό, the same, in that we interpret this sameness as a belonging-together. By this interpretation, do we not call upon the later definition of identity for help, according to which identity is the unity that unites something with itself?

But the statement of Parmenides speaks of thinking and of being. It speaks of the two that are indeed different, but precisely as the different are nonetheless the same. Here one might suppose that Parmenides already thinks ahead to that doubling of identity first thought in speculative idealism.

It is easy to interpret the sameness of thinking and being as named in the statement of Parmenides in the sense of identity as it is subsequently thought and familiar to us. What could prevent us from this? Nothing less than the statement itself that we read from Parmenides. It says: Being belongs with thinking in the same. Being is defined by an identity as a characteristic of identity. Contrary to this, identity as later thought is conceived as a

2. Parmenides, Fragment 3 in Hermann Diels, *Die Fragmente der Vorsokratiker*, vol. 1, 5th ed., ed. Walther Kranz (Berlin: Weidmannsche Buchhandlung, 1934), 231. English translation: Kathleen Freeman, ed. and trans., *Ancilla to the Pre-Socratic Philosophers* (Cambridge, Mass.: Harvard University Press, 1966), 42, translation modified.

basic characteristic of being. Therefore from the latter identity we could not claim to interpret the former identity through which even being itself is determined.

The sameness of thinking and being thought by Parmenides comes from further away than the identity conceived in metaphysics and which first stems from being.

The guiding word in the statement of Parmenides, τὸ αὐτό, the same, remains dark. We leave it dark. At the same time, however, we take a hint from the statement of Parmenides. Thus the path along which we ponder the essence of identity avoids arbitrariness.

In the meantime, however, we have indeed determined the sameness of thinking and being as the belonging-together of the two. We were too hasty, perhaps compelled. We must reverse this hastiness. We can do this if we do not take the belonging-together just mentioned for either the ultimate or even merely the authoritative interpretation of the sameness of thinking and being.

If we think the belonging-*together* in a customary manner then, as the emphasis of the word already indicates, the sense of belonging is determined by the together, i.e., by its unity. In such cases belonging means to be assigned to and classified under the gathering of a together, arranged within the unity of a manifold, placed together in the unity of a system, mediated in the uniting middle of a standardizing synthesis. Philosophy represents this belonging-*together* as *nexus* and *connexio,* as the necessary knotting of the one with the other.

This belonging-together, however, can also be thought as *belonging*-together. This signifies: the together is first defined by the belonging. Nevertheless, it still remains to be inquired here what "belonging" means and how first from this the "together" proper *to it* is determined. The answer lies closer to us than we imagine, but it does not lie at hand. It is enough for now if by means of this reference we note the possibility of no longer thinking belonging in terms of the unity of a together, but rather of thinking this together from belonging.

Yet does the reference to this possibility not exhaust itself in an empty wordplay, fabricating something that lacks any purchase in a verifiable state of affairs? It appears so until we look more keenly and let the matter speak.

The reference to belonging-together in the sense of *belonging*-together emerges from the perspective on a state of affairs already mentioned. It is only on account of its simplicity that it is difficult to keep in view. Meanwhile the state of affairs comes readily nearer to us when we observe the following: With the elucidation of belonging-*together* as *belonging*-together the discussion brings into view that sameness in which, according to the statement of Parmenides, thinking and being belong. Accordingly, we consider *belonging*-together from *what* belongs together there, namely thinking and being.

If we understand thinking as the privilege of the human, then the *belonging*-together of the human and being stands as our topic. Yet we see ourselves instantly compelled by the question: What does being mean? Who or what is the human? Everyone easily sees that without the adequate answering of these questions we lack the footing upon which we could discern something reliable about the *belonging*-together of thinking and being. As long as we question in this way, however, we remain trapped in the attempt to arrange and explain the coordination of the human and being as starting either from the human or from being. The footholds of the coordination remain the traditional conceptions of the human and being. We thus think in terms of the unity of a conceivable ordering together, one that is determined by either the human or being, instead of just for once attending to whether and how in this belonging-*together*, and above all else, a *belonging* could come into play. We stubbornly fail to hear that this *belonging*-together has already addressed us. To what extent is this the case?

The possibility of perceiving the claim of the *belonging*-together of the human and being, even if only from a distance, already arises when we more carefully ponder what is included under the current definitions of the essence of the human and of being.

Obviously the human is a kind of being. As such, he belongs in the whole of being. Belonging still means here classified under being. But as the thinking being [*Wesen*], the distinction of the human consists in his understanding the being of beings because, as addressed by being, he corresponds to this. The human *is* this relation of correspondence and he is only this. In the human essence there reigns a belonging to being, a belonging that hearkens to being because it is delivered into the ownership of this.

And being? Let us think being according to its inceptual sense as presencing [*An-wesen*]. Being does not presence for the human incidentally or as an exception. Rather, being essences and endures only in that it concernfully approaches [*an-geht*] the human. For it is the human, open for being, who first lets this arrive [*ankommen*] as presencing. Presencing *needs* the open of an illuminated clearing and is thereby transferred into the ownership of the human essence. This by no means says that being would be posited first or solely by the human. On the contrary, the following becomes clear:

The human and being are both pervaded by a belonging-to-one-another. From this *belonging*-together, which has not been considered more closely, the human and being have first received those essential definitions by which they are metaphysically conceptualized in philosophy.

Yet we never experience the prevailing *belonging*-together of the human and being as long as we reside within the mere representation of classifications and mediations. Such representing only ever shows us a knot that is tied from either being or the human and it thinks the *together* of the two as defined in this way. Representation does not let us enter into the *belonging*-together. How has it come to this? How can we experience this more closely? In this way, that we set ourselves apart from the bearing that merely conceives of such ties. This setting oneself apart [*Sichabsetzen*] is a principle [*Satz*] in the sense of a leap, one that leaps away, away from the current conception of the human as *animal rationale* and a subject for objects, away from being as the ground of beings.

Where does this leap of departure leap to, if it leaps away from the ground? Does it leap into an abyss? Yes, insofar as we still conceive the leap within the horizon of metaphysical thinking. No, insofar as we leap and let ourselves loose. To where? To there where we are already admitted: into a belonging to being, but to a being [*Sein*] that itself belongs to us, in that only *with* us can it *essence*, i.e., presence [an-*wesen*], *as* being.

Thus, in order to properly experience the *belonging*-together of the human and of being, a leap is necessary. This leap is the suddenness of a bridgeless entrance into that belonging which alone will allocate the reciprocality of the human and being and thus the constellation of the two. The leap is the sudden entrance into the realm from which being and the human have each time already reached one another in their essence.

A strange leap that presumably brings us the insight that we still do not sufficiently reside there where we authentically already are. Where are we? In which constellation of the human and being? Which *belonging*-together, which identity, and what kind, pervades the essence of being and the human? Out of what region does the claim of this identity, thought as *belonging*-together, speak?

Today it at least appears that one no longer requires laborious references, as was the case for years, to catch sight of the constellation in which the human and being belong together. One would like to imagine that it is enough to say the name "atomic age" in order to find out which being [*Sein*] it is that presences for us today. But are we allowed, then, to posit the technological world as at one with being? Apparently not, not even if we representatively understand this world as the whole of unleashed atomic energy together with the calculative planning and automatization that permeate all areas of human dwelling. Why does the reference to the technological world still not bring the contemporary constellation of the human and being into view? Because it thinks too briefly. For the whole of the technological world just mentioned is conceived in advance as something made by humans. The technological, taken in its broadest sense and in its manifold appearances, counts as the plan that the human projects, a plan that finally urges the human into the decision of whether he is to become a servant of his plan or to remain its master.

With this representation of the whole of the technological world, one winds everything back upon the human and, at best, arrives at the demand for an ethics of the technological world. Caught up in this conception, one opines that technology would be merely the affair of humans, no claim of being would speak in it. Obsessed with this opinion, we still do not even attend just once to the togetherness of the human and being, much less do we attempt to listen for the belonging that first extends both of these, the human and being, *to* one another.

For ourselves, let us finally set aside conceiving the technological merely technologically, i.e., starting from the human
and its machines. In this age, let us attend to the claim under
which there stands not only the human, but all beings, nature
and history, in respect to their being.

What claim do we mean? Our whole Dasein finds itself
everywhere challenged to take up the planning and calculating
of everything. What speaks in this challenge? Does it spring
from a self-made human whim? Or do not all beings already
only concern us insofar as they address us in their planability
and calculability? What comes to light here? Nothing less than
this: The human is challenged, i.e., positioned, to the same extent that being is. The being of beings is itself challenged, i.e.,
positioned, to let all beings presence in planability and calculability, first of all the human, so that he secures the beings that
concern him as the standing reserve for his planning and calculating, and that he drives this requisitioning interminably.
The claim that lets the being appear in planability and calculability and that also challenges the human into requisitioning
the beings that thereby appear, this claim constitutes the constellation in which we reside. The whole essence of the modern
technological world is determined by this.

The name for the gathering of the challenges that being and
the human deliver to each other such that they reciprocally
position one another is "positionality" [*das Ge-Stell*]. One is
unjustly jarred by this word. Instead of "placing" [*Stellen*] we
also say "setting" [*Setzen*] and find nothing wrong in our use
of the word "law" [*Gesetz*]. We understand the word "positionality" as corresponding to the word "law." Positionality is the
collection of standards [*Maßgabe*] for all setting, placing, and
ordering, wherein the human and being concernfully approach one another. Positionality lets the human and being
belong to each other in a bewildering manner. It is bewildering because we no longer find what positionality means
within the representational horizon that lets us think the
being of beings. For at one time, that which is to be thought in
the word "positionality" did not lie over against the human.
Positionality no longer concernfully approaches us [*geht
uns . . . an*] like being as presencing [*An-wesen*]. Positionality
first determines being in a togetherness with the human. But

what is to be thought in the word "positionality" is bewildering above all because it itself is nothing final, but first playfully solicits of us that which genuinely reigns through the contemporary constellation of the human and being.

The *belonging*-together of the human and being in the manner of a reciprocal challenging forth brings startlingly nearer to us both that and how the human is brought into the ownership of being and being is delivered into the ownership of the human essence. In positionality there reigns a bringing into ownership [*Vereignen*] and a delivering into ownership [*Zueignen*]. It is worth simply experiencing this owning [*Eignen*] wherein the human and being are appropriated [*ge-eignet*] to each other, i.e., enter into what we name the *event of appropriation* [Ereignis].

The word "event" [*Ereignis*] is taken from ordinary language. To appropriate [*Er-eignen*] means originally to eye [*er-äugen*], i.e., to catch sight of, to call into view, to take possession [*an-eignen*]. More originarily thought, the word "event" is now, as a guiding word, taken into the service of a thinking that attempts to keep in memory that dark word of Parmenides: τὸ αὐτό—the same is thinking and being. The word "event of appropriation" [*Ereignis*] can be translated just as little as the Greek guiding word λόγος or the Chinese *Tao*. The word event of appropriation here no longer means that which we otherwise name an occurrence, an incident. The word is now used as a *singulare tantum*.

Event of appropriation names the letting belong that is to be thought from it, and thus the authentic letting belong that brings the human and being into the ownership of each other. In positionality, what we experience as the essence of this constellation in the modern technological world is a prelude to what is called the event of appropriation. The event of appropriation does not necessarily or even merely remain in its prelude so as to let the human and being belong together in the manner of positionality. Rather, in the event of appropriation, the possibility arises that the event as the sheer reign of positionality is converted [*verwindet*] into a more inceptual appropriating. One such conversion of positionality from the event of appropriation—something never accomplishable by humans alone—would result in the appropriative retraction of the technological world from its position of mastery into one of servitude within a realm where the human more authentically reaches into the event of appropriation.

It appears as though we fell prey to the danger of all too casually directing our thinking toward some far-off universal, while under the name "event of appropriation" only what is the nearest of the near—that within which we already reside—immediately avows itself to us. But what could be nearer to us than that which brings us near to what we belong to—wherein we are what belongs—that is, the event of appropriation?

The beginning of this lecture issued the directive: attend to the path. Where has the path led? To the entrance of our thinking into what is simple, which we name the event of appropriation in a rigorous sense. It lets the human and being *belong* in a togetherness. Belonging now means brought into ownership, delivered into ownership. By his essence, because he is needed, the human is brought into the ownership of what is at first still called "being." As presencing, being is delivered into the ownership of the human essence.

Who we humans authentically are and what being authentically is, we may first duly question and surmise only when thinking has entered that region where appropriation [*Eignung*], bringing into ownership [*Vereignung*], propriety [*Eigentum*], and authenticity [*Eigentlichkeit*] reign, namely, in the event of appropriation [*Er-eignis*].

The event of appropriation is the realm, resonating in itself, through which the human and being reach one another in their essence, and achieve their essencing [*ihr Wesendes*] by losing those definitions that metaphysics has loaned to them.

To think the event of appropriation as event of appropriation means to work at building the structure of this realm. Thinking acquires the tool for building this self-suspending structure from language. For language is the most tender resonance, holding everything in this relation, in the suspended structure of the event of appropriation.

Indeed, what does that which has been said up to now have to do with the principle of identity? We answer by going back along the path traversed.

The event of appropriation brings the human and being into the ownership of their essential togetherness. We catch sight of a first appearance of this event, one compelling for us today, in positionality. But positionality constitutes the essence of the modern technological world. Positionality everywhere immediately approaches us. Positionality is, if we now be so permitted to speak, more extant than all atomic energy and all mechanical engineering, more extant than every form of organization, information, and automation. In positionality we catch sight of a belonging together of the human and being wherein the letting-belong first determines the type of togetherness and its unity. Positionality challenges the human to the calculation of being, itself arrogated into calculability. Positionality poises both the human and being to challenge each other into the requisitioning of beings as orderable standing reserve.

We were brought to the question of a belonging-together where the belonging takes precedence over the togetherness by the statement of Parmenides: "The same, namely, is thinking as well as also being." The question concerning the sense of this same, i.e., concerning the sameness of what is different, is the question concerning the essence of identity. According to the doctrine of metaphysics, identity holds as a basic characteristic of the being of beings. (The principle of identity says this as well, if we hear its formula A is A in its genuine intonation. Concerning the essence of identity, the principle of identity provides no information.) Contrary to this, the statement of Parmenides wherein identity itself speaks through the τὸ αὐτό, contains a hint. Yet the word τὸ αὐτό, the same, remains a riddle and remains so as long as thinking is not successful in thinking ahead to that region where belonging-*together* addresses us as *belonging*-together. In that region, one would experience the essential provenance of identity. Might we not search for the place of provenance of identity in what our thinking would like to come nearer to under the name "event of appropriation"?

The essence of identity is the propriety of the appropriative event [*Eigentum des Er-eignisses*]. We can only sensibly speak of authenticity when we think it in terms of the event of appropriation. If there could be something tenable in the attempt to point our thinking into the place of the essential provenance of identity, then what would become of the title of this lecture? The sense of the title "The Principle of Identity" would have changed.

The principle of identity first presents itself as a basic principle that says identity would be a characteristic of being, i.e., at the basis of beings. Along the way, this statement, in the sense of an expression, has become a principle in the manner of a leap that sets itself apart from being understood as the ground of beings and thus leaps into the abyss. Indeed this abyss is neither the empty nothing nor an obscure confusion, but rather the event of appropriation. In the event of appropriation, the essence of language resonates as that which speaks, that essence that once was named the house of being.[3]

Principle of identity now says: a leap that achieves the event of appropriation, i.e., the essence of identity, because the event needs it if the *belonging*-together of the human and being are otherwise to achieve the essential light of the event of appropriation.

On the way from principle as an expression about identity to the principle as a leap into the essential provenance of a *belonging*-together, thinking has transformed itself. Thus the thoughtful glance looks past the situation of humans in the present and catches sight of the constellation of being and the human from what first appropriates each to the other, from the event of appropriation.

Assuming the possibility would remain waiting for us that positionality, i.e., the challenging forth of the human and being into the calculability of the calculable, would be unveiled as the event of appropriation that first brings the human and being into the ownership of what is authentically their own, then this would clear a path along which the human would more inceptually experience beings, the whole of the modern technological world, nature and history, and, above all, the being of all of this.

As long as the contemporary meditation on the world of atomic energy, in all the seriousness of responsibility, only urges

---

3. Translator's Note: see "Brief über den 'Humanismus'" in *Wegmarken,* ed. Friedrich-Wilhelm von Herrmann, 3rd ed., *Gesamtausgabe,* vol. 9 (Frankfurt am Main: Vittorio Klostermann, 2004), 313–64, 313. English translation: "Letter on 'Humanism,'" trans. Frank A. Capuzzi, ed. and rev. William McNeill and David Farrell Krell, in *Pathmarks,* ed. William McNeill (Cambridge: Cambridge University Press, 1998), 239–76, 239.

for—and thereby satisfies itself with—pursuing the peaceful use of energy, contemplation remains standing at the halfway point. Consequently, the technological world in its metaphysical predominance is more deeply secured, and first rightly so.

Yet where was it determined that, forever into the future, nature would remain the nature of modern physics and history only present itself as an object of historiology? Indeed, we can neither discard the contemporary technological world as the devil's work, nor are we permitted to annihilate it, assuming it does not take care of this itself. Still less are we permitted to indulge in the opinion that the modern technological world would be the sort that just prohibits a leap of departure. This opinion emerges from the obsession with current events, which it holds to be the solely actual. This opinion is nevertheless fantastical, but not however the contemplation that looks toward what comes upon us as the claim of the essence of the identity of the human and being.

Whatever and however we attempt to think, we think in the play-space of a tradition. It reigns when, from out of our retrospective thinking, it releases us for a thinking ahead that is no longer a planning. Indeed only when we turn ourselves toward [zuwenden] what has already been thought will we be brought around to [verwendet; used for] what is yet to be thought.

Lecture IV

The following meditation passes over the last lecture, which discussed the principle of identity. Rather, this meditation recalls the course of the second lecture, admittedly now after the third, in order to traverse it once again toward other prospects. But because the lecture concerning the principle of identity is established in a particular manner as written and also as spoken,[1] a short afterword is required.

Long ago, thus in advance, it was already written. We find it in one of the dialogues of Plato that bears the name *Phaedrus*. Toward the end of this conversation, Socrates brings the discussion to the εὐπρέπεια καὶ ἀπρέπεια τῆς γραφῆς,[2] to what is seemly and unseemly of writing and the written. Socrates then recounts a story from Ancient Egypt.[3]

---

1. Translator's Note: Heidegger's lecture "The Principle of Identity" was recorded and published as a long-playing record by the Neske Verlag in 1958, *Martin Heidegger spricht den Vortrag zur Fünfhundertjahrfeier der Universität Freiburg im Breisgau "Der Satz der Identität."* The recording has been reissued on compact disc as Martin Heidegger, *Der Satz der Identität* (Stuttgart: Günther Neske, 1997).

2. Plato, *Phaidros*, in *Platonis Opera*, vol. 2, ed. John Burnet (Oxford: Oxford University Press, 1901), 274b6. English translation: *Phaedrus*, trans. Alexander Nehemas and Paul Woodruff, in *Plato: Complete Works*, ed. John M. Cooper and D. S. Hutchinson (Indianapolis, Ind.: Hackett Publishing Company, 1997), 506–56, 551.

3. ⟨Editor's note: For the spoken lecture, Heidegger declined to repeat this story, with the words ". . . that here cannot be recounted," for reasons of time. Among the manuscript materials, however, is found the

Socrates: Thus: I heard that in the region of Naucratis in Egypt, one of the old gods of the country is domiciled, to whom also belongs the sacred bird that they name the Ibis—the name of the god himself is Theuth. He is the first inventor of number and calculation, of geometry and astronomy, and further of the board and dice games, and above all of writing. At that time the king of the whole of Egypt was Thamus—he ruled in the great city of the upper region that the Greeks call the Egyptian Thebes, and the god: Ammon. Theuth came to him and showed him his arts and explained that it was necessary to allow all Egyptians to take part in them. Thamus, however, asked about the use of each art and, as Theuth gave his explanations, Thamus meted out praise or censure according to whether a description pleased or displeased him. Thamus is supposed to have expressed much to Theuth in both directions about each of the arts—it would be too laborious to repeat it all. But when he came to writing: "This, O King," Theuth said then, "this knowledge will make the Egyptians wiser and strengthen their memory; for it was invented as an aid to memory and wisdom." But he objected: "Oh you masterful technician, Theuth! To one goes the capacity to invent skills in technical arts, but indeed to another that of passing judgment as to what harm or benefit they bring to those who are supposed to use them. Even you as father of writing have now, out of affection, proclaimed the opposite of what it is capable. For it will produce forgetfulness in the soul of those who learn it through neglect of the memory—from trust in writing they will recollect externally, through foreign figures, not internally from what is their own. Thus you have invented an aid not for memory but for recollecting. Of wisdom, however, you administer to the pupils only the appearance, not the truth; for knowing much without instruction, they will appear to be full of insight, while for the most part they are without insight and difficult in dealings—having become someone apparently wise, instead of someone wise."

Phaedrus: Oh, Socrates—whether from Egypt or wherever else you like, how effortlessly you produce stories!

---

following translation by Heidegger of *Phaedrus* 274c5–275b4, inserted here.)

In the course of reflecting on this story, Socrates says to Phaedrus (275c5–d6).

SOCRATES: Whoever now is of the opinion that he could leave his art ⟨namely that of speech⟩ behind in something written, and also he who takes it ⟨what is written⟩ up again as though something clear and reliable would come forth from what has been written, each of them is totally naive and has in truth no knowledge of the pronouncement of the god Ammon, if he believes that written speech would be useful for something other than facilitating the one who knows ⟨namely, the one who already knows what the writing wants to say⟩ in again coming across what is written.

Phaedrus remarks of the words quoted by Socrates only: Ὀρθότατα; "Quite right." Socrates continues:

SOCRATES: There is somehow something uncanny, my Phaedrus, in writing and in what is written itself and in this it is truly like painting. For in this, too, its figures stand there as though alive, but if you ask them anything, they are augustly and wholly silent. Written speeches, however, also do the same. You might be of the opinion that they said something about what they consider, so to speak, but when you ask with the intention of finding out something of what they say: ἕν τι σημαίνει μόνον ταὐτὸν ἀεί—a certain one repeatedly announces only one and the same thing ⟨it sticks to an indeterminate monotony⟩. Once written down, however, every speech roams about everywhere, just as much with those to whose ears they belong as with those that they do not concern. The written speech on its own admittedly does not know to whom it should speak and to whom it should not. And if the speech is mishandled or even mischievously berated, then it always needs its father as its helper. For it is neither able to defend nor help itself.

Through the conversation between Socrates and his young friend Phaedrus, Plato himself speaks. He, the poetic master of the thoughtful word, indeed speaks here only of writing, but indicates at the same time what always came over him ever anew throughout his whole path of thought, namely that what is thought in thinking cannot be expressed. Indeed, it would be too hasty to conclude that therefore what is thought would be unspeakable. Rather, Plato knew that it would be the task of thinking to bring the unsaid near to thinking by means of a saying, and to bring it near precisely as the issue that is to be thought. Thus even in what is written by him, what Plato thought is never there to be read directly, even though there are written conversations, but because we too greedily and erroneously search for a doctrine we are only rarely able to release these conversations into the pure movement of a concentrated thinking.

It is now necessary to link this meditation to the second lecture. At its beginning was said: "In some way we all think and nevertheless are all inexperienced with the issue of whether and how grounding-principles move thinking or even bring it to rest." This remark understood the word "grounding-principles" already in the transformed sense of leaps into the abyss; "move thinking"—this means to build a path for thinking; "bring to a rest"—this means to bring to where all movement is first gathered, not in order to end, but rather to begin from the source. Indeed we are—all of us—inexperienced in what is demanded of thinking, if it should otherwise find a way out of its ensnarement in calculation and dialectic. Both of these, calculative and dialectical thinking, are at ground the same, namely in terms of that ground that the principle of reason [*Satz vom Grund*] names, without however thinking its essence. Yet enough is already gained if our focus turns to the inexperience just mentioned. The path of these lectures may bring us to this.

The second lecture named the signpost. Upon it was to be read "logic." The doctrine of thinking is called such. If we read the signpost carefully enough it leads us far from all that we would expect. At first we followed the signpost without attending more closely to what was characteristic of the indicated path. To be sure, it must have been obvious that we lost ourselves, or so it seemed, in refining the significance of the equivocality in the title "Basic Principles of Thinking." In fact, refining the significance of the title is the sole task. Admittedly, we must obviate the misunderstanding that believes it would just be a matter of showing the ways in which the different meanings of the words composing the title could be understood. Behind the equivocality of the title "Basic Principles of Thinking" is concealed a back-and-forth of questioning that concerns thinking insofar as this, thinking, pervades our essence, i.e., the relation of being in itself to us. Experienced in this way, thinking means letting be, namely letting the being be in its being. So experienced, thinking also first gives a playspace to poetizing. So experienced, thinking requires for itself a way of its own [*eine eigene Weise*], more in the sense of a melody, the performers of which are called thinkers.

The questions that are hidden in the title "Basic Principles of Thinking" require an answer that says how we hold ourselves in thinking, in what way we let ourselves into thinking and engage with thinking, what paths leading there already stand open, what paths into the releasement of thinking are first to be hewn, what paths must then be built. Such questions grow from the supposition that, at a time that we cannot know, a still-higher determination in the essential destiny of being is reserved for thinking. How much contemporary efforts can do for this, or better can leave off from doing, no one knows. Many, even most, indications are that the devastation of Dasein into an always merely calculative thinking will continue to increase. To imagine that nihilism would be overcome is probably the fundamental error of the present age. Nietzsche's saying, written a few years before his mental collapse in Turin, remains true. It reads: "Nihilism stands at the door; where does this most uncanny of all guests come from?"[4] Even today one still evades the question of the essential place of origin of this guest and thereby first opens the doors for this guest to both the East and the West in equal measure; for both worlds are incapable of addressing one another from the dimension that each would first have to be released into, so as to experience both what is and from which essence of being it is that all beings speak.

---

4. Friedrich Nietzsche, *Der Wille zur Macht*. I. Buch, "*Der europäische Nihilismus*," in *Nietzsche's Werke*, Großoktavausgabe, vol. 15: *Ecce Homo. Der Wille zur Macht*, 3rd ed. (Leipzig: Alfred Kröner, 1922), §1, 141. Friedrich Nietzsche, *Der Wille zur Macht*, ed. Peter Gast and Elisabeth Förster-Nietzsche, 13th ed. (Stuttgart: Alfred Kröner Verlag, 1996), 7. English translation: Friedrich Nietzsche, *The Will to Power*, ed. Walter Kaufmann, trans. Walter Kaufmann and R. J. Hollingdale (New York: Vintage Books, 1968), 7.

The attempt at a clarification of the equivocality in the title "Basic Principles of Thinking" gives the impression that this would concern a preliminary and external business. Thought in terms of the issue at stake, however, something else is at play.

The contemplation of the title does not dismantle the given words and concepts into their elements of significance. The lecture discusses the place in which our thinking belongs. In order to recognize this intention clearly and to know it cumulatively [*gesammelt*], it is advisable now to look back in a unified manner over what was previously gone through, so that the view along the path to the place of thinking might broaden and its obscurity diminish.

Should we risk speaking more pointedly, then it could be said: The sole issue of the lectures is their title. Nothing stands under the title, nothing in the sense of a collection of utterances about a topic. Nothing stands under the title because everything lies therein. The title, therefore, is likewise no title; it is not a heading [*Überschrift*], but rather a *postscript* [Nachschrift]. Fraught with all the dubiousness of the written, it writes something out that follows upon our thinking, and this means it would like to come near and nearer to our thinking, in that it attempts to transform what is written back into something heard, and that which is heard, however, into something caught sight of. For only what we have caught sight of do we see, do we preserve as what has been seen (the beautiful). We only know what has been seen, knowing taken in the ancient sense that says: having seen and retaining what was seen, namely as something that continually regards us. What Plato thinks by the word ἰδέα has its origin in such an experience. For thought in a Greek manner, the "idea" is that outward appearance of things from which they regard us, the humans. But we would still not be thinking all of this in a sufficiently Greek manner were we to interpret the relations of outward appearing and regarding [*Aussehen und Ansehen*] merely optically in terms of the sense of sight. Outward appearance in the sense of ἰδέα is no rigid vision, but rather the wafting of χάρις, of grace. What Hölderlin in an elegy sings of his countrymen hits upon the essence of the Greek relation of humans to the being of beings, as poetized by Plato.

Hölderlin says:

[. . .] and to breathe in this grace,
as is fitting [*geschickliche*], is granted them by a divine spirit.[5]

What is the point of this digression? It is not one, but instead just the ever newly necessary thoughtful recollection of what is essencing of being [*das Wesende des Seins*], the breath of which we no longer detect when we poke around in the defunct concepts of philosophy without thereby noticing that a word like idea and ἰδέα still speaks if thinking duly hearkens toward it. Admittedly it all too often appears futile today to once again open a view to these simple relationships and thus at the same time to show how they shine through the whole of Western thinking up to the grandiose concluding section of Hegel's *Logic*, which bears the heading "The Idea."

As long as we close our view into the simple shining of being—hindered by what we have merely read about, hardened by theories, hastily satisfied with doctrinal opinions, enchanted by the plethora of daily novelties—for just so long will our thinking go without rootedness in the soil, for just so long will it lack the precondition that would allow for us to come near, even if only approximately, to the realm that the discussion of the basic principles of thinking attempts to point out.

The equivocality of the talk of "Basic Principles of Thinking" is threefold: 1. A double meaning; 2. An ambiguity; 3. A transformation of sense.

If we think through the threefold equivocality at once, we arrive not only at the tradition of the history of thinking, but rather this tradition liberates us for another appropriation of its essence. Thus if what has already been said is at points intentionally repeated, then we may observe: The repetition of the same into what is each time more inceptual belongs to the art of thinking.

Let us consider the first kind of equivocality in the talk of the "Basic Principles of Thinking": the doubled meaning.

---

5. Friedrich Hölderlin, "Stutgard. An Siegfried Schmidt," in *Sämtliche Werke*, historisch-kritische Ausgabe, vol. 4: *Gedichte 1800–1806*, ed. Norbert von Hellingrath, 2nd ed. (Berlin: Propyläen Verlag, 1923), 114–18, 114. English translation: Friedrich Hölderlin, "Stuttgart. To Siegfried Schmidt," in *Poems & Fragments*, ed. and trans. Michael Hamburger (London: Anvil Press Poetry, 1994), 254–61, 254; translation modified.

Grammatically represented, it concerns the genitive. Accordingly, "Basic Principles of Thinking" means on the one hand: Basic principles for thinking. Taken thus, the basic principles are those laws to which thinking remains subordinated as their object. On the other hand, the genitive speaks as *genitivus subiectivus*. According to this, the basic principles are the regulations posited by thinking itself. The positing proceeds through the I that, as subject, thinks the object. The double meaning of the genitive indicates: thinking is at the same time the subject and the object for its basic principles considered as rules. Thinking is the object of itself as subject. We must first look past the rigid and truly inadequate grammatical distinctions regarding the genitive for there to appear before our eyes the state of affairs from out of which the phrase "Basic Principles *of* Thinking" speaks.

What state of affairs? Thinking approaches itself in its basic principles as posited by itself and thereby illuminates itself. Thinking goes and stands in a light that, to all appearances, it itself has ignited. Yet at the same time thinking thereby enters a shadow that, by virtue of the capacities loaned to thinking each time, it can never catch sight of. Even the relation of thinking to itself in regard to its place of origin lies in a shadow for thinking. Thinking pursues this—through every relation back to itself—always from behind, just as though thinking itself cast this shadow. Thinking does cast it and the shadow is thus first cast to thinking. In the nigh tedious double meaning of the genitive "Basic Principles *of* Thinking" the relations between illumination and shadowing are concealed. They pervade thinking, but they themselves are scarcely considered, they could not be, so long as thinking is designated an activity of the soul, of the spirit, of the subject, of the human, and is thereby cut off from and truncated in regard to its relationship to being wherein it is at home. With respect to this truncation of thinking—something remarked in many respects and nevertheless not relinquished, but instead even held fast to—all dialectic is the attempt to complete it, that is, to define thinking by the whole of its rationally understood essence. But this whole ultimately remains the shadowless light of reason and of the subjectivity that knows itself absolutely. And wherever the shadow is seen, it is only understood as the limit of brightness. But the shadow is something more and other than a limit.

The saying of Leonardo's: Light reveals, shadow conceals,[6] comes closer to the state of affairs. Yet the decisive question must search for the originary unity of disclosure and concealment. To be sure, thinking has been brought into a relationship with light since days of old. One speaks of the natural light of reason. In deference to the definition of illumination and enlightenment, which one accords to reason and to thinking, one has forgotten the shadowing from which thinking stems. This shadowing arises neither from a realm of shades and ghosts, nor is it dispatched with the cheap remark that next to the rational there would also be the irrational; for the irrational always remains the stillborn child of rationalism.

The presiding and ultimately completely overpowering relation of thinking to light, to illumination, and to shining shows itself early on in that a character of thinking was recognized called reflection. This means, on the one hand, a bending back upon the self. Insofar as thinking as representation represents something, thinking appears to itself in a certain manner in what is represented by it and therein finds the occasion to bend itself back upon its representing, to re-flect. Let us note some everyday examples: When we look at the familiar jug or some other thing, the apple on the plate, the pipe on the wicker chair, and thereby only note what is optically given, then this shows that these objects present themselves to us ever only in a particular aspect. The particular aspect depends on the vantage point from which we look upon the objects. This vantage point is a way of our representing. The particular aspect of the object lets us reflect upon our vantage point. It seems as though the object would be an X, around which a collection of aspects can take shape and must take shape in order to completely capture it.

---

6. Cf. Leonardo da Vinci, *Das Buch von der Malerei*, Deutsche Ausgabe nach dem Codex Vaticanus 1270, ed. and trans. Heinrich Ludwig (Vienna: Wilhelm Braumüller, 1882), Part Five, "Von Schatten und Licht," Nr. 549 (550), 277. English translation: Leonardo da Vinci, *Treatise on Painting*, vol. 1: *Translation*, ed. and trans. A. Philip McMahon (Princeton, N.J.: Princeton University Press, 1956), Part Five, "Of Shadow and Light," Nr. 577, 209. Translator's Note: "Shadow is of the nature of darkness; illumination is of the nature of light. One conceals, the other reveals."

Nevertheless, if we think of the mentioned objects as things, if we experience them commemoratively, then they do not refer us to our vantage points and representations, instead they hint at a world from out of which they are what they are. When, for example, Cézanne lets the *montagne St. Victoire* appear in his paintings again and again and the mountain presences as the mountain ever more simply and powerfully, then this does not lie solely, nor even primarily, in that Cézanne discovers himself ever more decisively through his painterly technique, but rather in that the "topic" moves, i.e., speaks, ever more simply. The artist is capable of hearing this claim more purely each and every time such that this claim guides the brush for him and even proffers the colors to him. The painter paints what he hears as the appeal of the essence of things. All art, not only poetry, moves in the realm that speaks as language and requires something besides a reflection on objects and the representation of the same. However, to the extent that thinking is now experienced as representation, which poses what presences both before itself and toward itself, there belongs to thinking a return relation to itself, a reflection. As a consequence of the self-unfolding dominance of reflection, the being first becomes an object. On the other hand, and more poignantly, reflection means the shining back upon thinking of what is thought in thinking and, conversely, of thinking upon what is thought. This shining in itself of thinking, intimated in Plato's interpretation of being as ἰδέα, first comes completely to the fore for thinking as soon as reflection in the initial sense mentioned above comes fully into play in all possible regards. This occurs where the subjectivity of the subject is thought absolutely, in speculative idealism. The meager distinction between a *genitivus subiectivus* and *obiectivus* in the talk of "Basic Principles of Thinking" first comes to life and reveals what it properly names when we think ahead to the reflection-character of representing.

All thinking, in some way, even if as yet undefined, is a thinking of itself and is nevertheless no mere self-mirroring. In accordance with the return relation to itself that is characteristic of it, thinking can revolve around itself, at times in a lofty sense, at times in a superficial one; ultimately, in the grand style, thinking itself can even draw the circle along which it revolves around itself in its orbiting.

Along a long and convoluted path, Western-European thinking finally and wittingly reached the ambit of light formed by it and its reflection-character. This light-dimension is speculative dialectics that, after the precedent of Kant, develops itself into a system in the thinking of Fichte, Schelling, and Hegel. The system to be contemplated here would remain misunderstood were we to represent it as merely a woven net of concepts thrown over actuality. As "the thought" [*der Gedanke*] the system is being itself, dissolving all beings in itself and thus sketching out the preliminary form of what now comes to the fore as the essence of the technological world.

That the world stamped by the metaphysics of Karl Marx can become a—I say "a," not "the" and not "the authentic"— gathering ground for the whole of the modern technological world is founded on the essence of the issue at stake. For the metaphysics of Karl Marx depends more decisively than one thinks on the speculative idealism of the metaphysics of Hegel, and depends here in the most decisive form of dependence, namely that of mere antagonism. This appears in that the metaphysics of Marxism remains dialectics and must so remain. The dialectic and its system, here and there, are no contrived houses of concepts, but rather life and actuality; they are also this even if in an entirely different way for the pair of poets who are also friends of the speculative thinkers Fichte, Schelling, and Hegel— for Hölderlin and Novalis. In their "night songs," both have seen that dark light wherein the rational brightness of absolute logic is cancelled, but at the same time presupposed and confirmed.[7]

---

7. Translator's Note: For Hölderlin's "Night Songs," see his December 8, 1803, letter to the publisher Friedrich Wilmans, where the poet refers to a forthcoming collection of nine poems—"Chiron," "Thränen," "An die Hoffnung," "Vulkan," "Blödigkeit," "Ganymed," "Hälfte des Lebens," "Lebensalter," and "Der Winkel von Hahrdt"—as his "Night Songs." Letter 243 in Friedrich Hölderlin, *Sämtliche Werke*, Stuttgarter Hölderlin Ausgabe, vol. 6: 1, *Briefe*, ed. Adolf Beck (Stuttgart: W. Kohlhammer Verlag, 1954), 436. The poems are translated together in one place under the heading "Night Songs" in Friedrich Hölderlin, *Odes and Elegies*, trans. Nick Hoff (Middletown, Conn.: Wesleyan University Press, 2008), 165–83. For Novalis's "Night Songs," see his "Hymnen an die Nacht," in *Schriften: Die Werke Friedrich von Hardenbergs*, vol. 1: *Das dichterische Werke*, ed. Paul Kluckhohn and Richard Samuel with Heinz Ritter and Gerhard Schulz

The reflection-character of thinking and its development into dialectic belong together. Both of them, as well as their belonging together, are rooted in the fact that Western thinking, already at its dawn, was cast such that founding and calculating in the broadest sense took priority.

Our historical consciousness is quick to present the dialectic of speculative idealism as the product of a rationality positing itself absolutely. One can explain this dialectic as theologically unworthy of belief. One can, following Kierkegaard's judgment, suspect speculative idealism of a still-higher swindle, but one thing remains: Speculative dialectic thoroughly dominates today's world reality, whether out in the open or hidden, conceived or caricatured, ossified or renovated. Behind the harmless double meaning of the genitive "Basic Principles of Thinking" lies concealed the power of reflective-dialectical thinking, which, in the meantime, though originally European, has multifariously spread across the entire earth.

With this we are referred to the second form of equivocality in the talk of "Basic Principles of Thinking." What is meant is the ambiguity in the talk of thinking as such [*dem Denken*]. Now, with a glance back to what was said, this can be made univocal. "Thinking as such" is nowhere to be found. Every thinking bears its dispensational stamp. "Basic Principles of Thinking" can consequently only mean that thinking into which we were sent long ago. Let us note in passing that the belief in a commonplace thinking, universal only by appearances and supposedly the same throughout all ages, is one of the sources for the rise of nihilism and the tenacity of its imperceptible powers of asserting itself into all regions of the world.

As soon as we get involved with the basic principles of thinking and ponder these, we see ourselves compelled to experience our thinking just once in its essential provenance so as to be properly there where, as thinking beings [*denkende Wesen*], for a long time we already are. The path into this experience is pointed out to us by the signpost we have mentioned several

---

(Stuttgart: W. Kohlhammer Verlag, 1960), 130–57. English translation: *Hymns to the Night*, trans. Dick Higgins (Kingston, N.Y.: McPherson & Co., 1988).

times. Upon this we read the name "logic," which indicates that thinking is defined as λόγος. Nevertheless, this reference itself remains suspended in indeterminacy as long as we cannot show why and in what way it comes about that the main characteristic of thinking is found in the λόγος. That this is so need not count as self-evident or natural. It is a fate that determines the world each time in a different way, as much the scholastic world of the Middle Ages as that of modern science and, ultimately, the technological world of today. This fate harbors in itself the question of whether logic ultimately, i.e., justly, directs the regiment concerning thinking or whether thinking still has not been brought under the protection of the λόγος and its yet-to-be-unfolded essence, as is its due.

Restricting ourselves, we here only mention the following: To what extent has thinking, defined by λόγος, anything to do with what one names the "basic principles of thinking"? This connection is obviously only a possible and necessary one in that our thinking is of a fundamental [*grundsätzlicher*] kind, in the literal sense, which says that the λόγος as such has the character of a grounding-principle. To what extent does it behave this way? In answering this, we must settle for a few references. The verb for the noun λόγος runs λέγειν and means "to read," in the sense of gathering, laying together. Aristotle sketches the λόγος of logic as the λόγος ἀποφαντικός, that laying together whose capacity is such that, through what is laid together—the path is long—it lets appear what was already-lying-together-before—the long path as such. This basic form of thinking Aristotle also simply names ἀπόφανσις. The word in its naming power is not to be translated; it means the bringing-to-appearance, here from itself, of what is already lying before. When we translate the word ἀπόφανσις by exposition, we indeed stress the letting lie before, but what is characteristically Greek—the bringing-to-shine—is lost.

If we attend to what was remarked concerning Plato's ἰδέα, which defines the presence of what presences, i.e., being, as outward appearing and regarding, then the correct interrelation of ἰδέα and ἀπόφανσις as being and thinking leaps into view, assuming our sheerly historiological knowledge about philosophy has not become too stupid to still see this startling state of affairs in its simplicity and never again forget its face.

What is most peculiar in what has come to pass in the essential history of Western thinking is that the characteristic of the λόγος of logic that bears everything, the ἀπόφανσις, the disclosive bringing-to-appearance, just as soon disappears and indeed in favor of the other model of the λόγος that is originally native to ἀπόφανσις. Aristotle brings this concisely and succinctly to light when he circumscribes the λόγος as λέγειν τι κατά τινος.[8] Literally translated, this says: to expose something in the direction of something, namely toward that upon-which and about-which the exposition comes when it directs itself toward what is present. This about-which both underlies and lies before the exposition. Spoken in an example: The long path is what lies before, what is presented in the λόγος ἀποφαντικός "The path is long." The "long" is not added to the "path," as the linguistic form of the expression would like to persuade us, but rather is properly laid together with the long path, whereby the path shows itself as what lies before. The path comes to the fore as long.

It appears as though the talk would be of trivial matters; of trivial matters, no, but of simple matters whose weight is scarcely estimable. The ever-newly necessary reference to the distinction between the trivially common and the bewilderingly simple hits upon the plight of our thinking, which prevents it from correctly finding its way into the space of freedom. Today, to a certain degree one is used to the fact that where the most violent machinery and intricate devices produce something useful, these results alone count as discoveries, while, on the contrary, plain insight into a simple state of affairs counts for nothing. This is noteworthy; but what is noteworthy here is a primordial custom of human opining that what is the feat of one's own doing easily counts more than the gift of a call [An-rufes] or a sighting [Anblickes]. Thus it is only with difficulty that we find the right sense

---

8. Cf. Aristotle, *Analytica Priora*, I, 1; 24 a 16 sq. Aristoteles, *Analytica Priora et Posteriora*, ed. W. D. Ross (Oxford: Oxford University Press, 1964). English translation: Aristotle, *Prior Analytics*, trans. A. J. Jenkinson, in *The Complete Works of Aristotle*, 2 vols., ed. Jonathan Barnes (Princeton, N.J.: Princeton University Press, 1995), vol. 1: 39–113, 39. Translator's Note: Jenkinson's translation of the passage in question reads: "A proposition, then, is a statement affirming or denying something of something" (39).

for this quiet incident whereby with this definition of the λόγος of logic, i.e., of thinking, its all-bearing character just as soon withdraws. When the ἀπόφανσις-character vanishes into forgetfulness, i.e., that thinking is a letting appear—something that occurred long ago—then the version of λόγος just mentioned presses into the foreground: the λέγειν τι κατά τινος. This is subsequently dissociated from the expositive-character and conceived on its own as relation. Thus we find ourselves transposed into the long-accepted conception of the λόγος of logic: It is the connection of a subject, "the path," with a predicate, "long." This conception of the λόγος is even correct; its correctness can be proven everywhere by grammatical inspection.

The states of affairs now mentioned at first look like themes for a historiological pedantry recounting the history of logic. In truth, however, something uncanny occurs with the entirely unobtrusive retreat and disappearance of the ἀπόφανσις-character in λόγος—this is said without exaggeration. What happens? The course becomes clear for the development of thinking as calculating, founding, concluding. The modern technological world likewise rests on this, the essence of which we will never be able to think through so long as we do not engage in a meditation that shows what lies resolved in the casting of thinking as λόγος, in this disappearance of the ἀπόφανσις-character. That the λόγος so stamped becomes the fate of the modern technological world is just one thing. The other, which is prepared in the withdrawal of the ἀπόφανσις-character, approaches us still more essentially. We can first ponder this by following the signpost still more decisively and further back, the signpost that says that thinking would be defined by λόγος; for we cannot concern ourselves now with the consequences of the withdrawal of the ἀπόφανσις-character. We find ourselves much more called into the question of what this disappearing of the inceptual self-showing essence of λόγος authentically . . . is, and here and now still is.

By this question we proceed along a perhaps somewhat tangential path, in that we discuss the equivocality of the talk of "Basic Principles of Thinking." In the meantime, the second kind of equivocality, namely the ambiguity of the talk of thinking "as such," has contracted itself into a univocality.

Thinking "as such"—this is our Western thinking, defined from the λόγος and calibrated to this. On no account does this mean that the world of ancient India, China, and Japan would remain thought-less. Much more, the reference to the λόγος-character of Western thinking contains for us the behest that before touching upon these foreign worlds, should we risk it, we first ask ourselves whether we at all have the ear to hear what is thought there. This question becomes all the more burning as European thinking also threatens to become planetary, in that the contemporary Indians, Chinese, and Japanese in many cases report their experiences to us only in our European way of thinking. Thus from there and from here everything is stirred up in a gigantic mishmash wherein it is no longer discernible whether or not the ancient Indians were English empiricists and Lao Tzu a Kantian. Where and how is there supposed to be an awakening conversation calling each back into its own essence, if on both sides substancelessness has the final word?

The univocality pondered just now in the talk of thinking "as such," however, first becomes complete when it clarifies to what extent this thinking is not only dependent upon basic principles, but at the same time is itself likewise directed to properly heed these basic principles as such, to meditate [*meditieren*] on them. *Meditare* is the same word that stands in our loan word *Medizin* [medicine]; *medear* means to attend to something, to healingly care. One of the oldest pronouncements of a Greek thinker, that of Periander, runs: μελέτα τὸ πᾶν.⁹ Take into care the whole of beings: Consider being!

Thinking holds itself to the basic principles and considers these properly because the simple jointure of the λόγος already has the character of a grounding-principle. This proclamation loses what is bewildering about it only when we think the word "basic-principle" in a Greek manner and that means from the intact essence of the λόγος as λόγος ἀποφαντικός.

Principle [*Satz*] is called in Greek θέσις. We are familiar with the word from the language of speculative idealism whose dialectic can be characterized by thesis, antithesis,

9. Hermann Diels, *Die Fragmente der Vorsokratiker*, ed. Walther Kranz, vol. I, 5th ed. (Berlin: Weidmann, 1934), 65. "The Seven Wisemen," Periander, Fragment 10 (73a),ζ. English translation: Diogenes Laertius, "Periander," ch. 7 of *Lives of Eminent Philosophers*, vol. 1, ed. and trans. R. D. Hicks (Cambridge, Mass.: Harvard University Press, 1991), 103. Hicks's translation reads "Practice makes perfect" (103).

synthesis. Here, however, the word "thesis," proposition, has the sense of spontaneity, the deed, the practical deed [*Tathandlung*]. We think of Fichte, who said: The I posits the not-I.[10] In the Greek word θέσις something else obtains. Θέσις means letting lie before: that which lies before. This letting is admittedly no mere passivity, much more a doing and indeed of a more original and higher kind than could ever be thought and performed by the modern concept of thesis, of positing.

In the later history of thinking, the λόγος ἀποφαντικός will often be defined as a simple proposition, though this is sooner grasped grammatically from predication, namely as the interweaving and tying together of the propositional subject and the propositional predicate. All of this was already prepared for by Plato and Aristotle, something which cannot be treated here, where it is a matter of characterizing the simple proposition as a basic principle, and of doing so from θέσις understood in a Greek manner. The λόγος ἀποφαντικός is an exposition that lays together. It is θέσις as a letting lie before, namely of that which already lies before and thus lies at the ground of the presentation. Here ground means as much as soil [*Boden*]. We speak of the earth's soil [*Erdboden*], of the ocean floor [*Meeresboden*]. The peasant knows the poor soils within his fields, ground that only produces stunted growth. In the example, what lies before is "the long path," the basis and ground that the proposition "the path is long" lets lie before and thereby brings to appearance. Ground here means so much as what is each time present. Every simple proposition that lets something present lie before is a grounding-statement [*Grund-Satz*] in the sense here elucidated.

But how does it stand with those basic principles that are called such in an extraordinary manner, and this precisely

10. Cf. J. G. Fichte, *Grundlage der gesamten Wissenschaftslehre* (1794), in *Sämtliche Werke*, vol. 1, ed. I. H. Fichte (Berlin: Verlag von Veit und Comp, 1845), 103. J. G. Fichte, *Grundlage der gesammten Wissenschaftslehre als Handschrift für seine Zuhörer,* in *Werke,* 1793–1795, ed. Reinhard Lauth and Hans Jacob with Manfred Zahn, *Gesamtausgabe* I.2 (Stuttgart-Bad Cannstatt: Friedrich Frommann Verlag [Günther Holzboog], 1964), 249–451, 265–66. English translation: *Science of Knowledge,* ed. and trans. Peter Heath and John Lachs (Cambridge: Cambridge University Press, 1982), 103.

because they are not arbitrary, simple statements like the given example: "The path is long" or "The sky is blue"? In which sense could the principle of identity or the principle of reason, still be called basic principles according to what has now been said? In what relation do they stand to ordinary statements? The basic principles, conventionally so designated, seemingly concern every statement as statement and that means that at the same time they concern what an ordinary statement posits: namely what lies at the ground and what lies before. What the principle of identity posits, identity, does not lie before, how-ever, like the path, the mountain, the tree, the creek, etc. Iden-tity is not something present, no ground and soil in this sense. But everything that is present as such, that is, everything that is in presence, is itself the same as itself. Identity belongs in presence as such; we never encounter it as something among other present things. But then can presence, which itself is nothing present, still be called a ground in the way that some-thing present is? Not only can it, it must be so called and has been so called for a long time; for what would something pres-ent ever be, were it not grounded in presence? What would all grounds and soils be, if that grounding did not reign in them, which encounters everything that lies before precisely in its lying before, everything that presences in its presencing? If we were once capable of thinking what is named in the word "pres-ence" according to the entire fullness and breadth that blos-somed in the Greek experience of the world, then and only then would we be permitted to say instead of presence also: *being*. Otherwise—i.e. without the heartful, fulfilled, and thor-oughly considered commemoration of the destiny of being from the Greek world—the word "being" remains an empty sound, a deaf nut, or the name of a confused representation.

The specially named basic principles pertain to the being of beings. But for a long time now, being has been thought as ground, sometimes more, sometimes less decisively and clearly. It comes to light here that this word "ground" is itself ambiguous, insofar as, on the one hand, in regard to what lies before, it signi-fies the presencing soil and ground, and on the other hand, what is meant is not something present, but rather presence itself. The basic principles are principles of the being of beings. These basic principles, however, are also called basic principles of thinking and indeed of the thinking that determines itself from the λόγος ἀποφαντικός. By following the signpost, we reached the univocality of the talk of "Basic Principles of Thinking." At the same time, however, this univocality transposed us into the midst of the clash of questions that motivate the entirety of Western thinking, precisely because this is defined by the λόγος. These questions run: Do the basic principles of thinking hold because they are principles of being as the ground of beings? Or are they the latter because, as laws of thinking, they first posit what lies before in its lying before, what presences in its presence, and thus first of all establish being? Or are the basic principles of thinking at the same time the basic principles of being? What does "at the same time" then mean here? Are the basic principles of the two in a harmony or a discord? Or does even such questioning directed at the basic principles of thinking not yet reach the center of the issue? What issue? It is the issue of Western thinking, an issue that is in itself conflictual. Conflicted is namely the privilege between thinking and being, conflicted, whether and how the one reigns over the other, or whether they are even of the same rank. Thinking has not yet concerned itself with this possibility. In the case where thinking and being are supposed to be of equal rank—could a settlement ever be satisfactory, especially when it is to be reached by a third party that would either have to reign over or subtend both of these and accordingly remain what is primary before the two? This would be something to ponder, assuming that the conflict between being and thinking for the priority of one over the other has not previously been settled. But even then, if this conflict between thinking and being were to be an essential one, the primordial conflict, as it were, then precisely then would our thinking have to find a path upon which we could first come to experience and recognize this primordial conflict as such.

Indeed, we are already moving along this path. The signpost brought us along it; it showed: logic is the doctrine of thinking because the latter is defined as λόγος. Yet we go further along the indicated path and ask: Why and in what way does it come about that the basic trait of thinking is found in λόγος?

Thinking lets what is present appear in its presencing, adheres to presencing, to the being of beings, to the ground. And this? At the dawn of Western thinking, namely for Heraclitus, being itself was unveiled as Λόγος. The particulars of this are shown in another place.[11]

In the thinking of Heraclitus the word Λόγος already speaks simultaneously as the name for being and for thinking. Λόγος is the one and only word for being and for thinking; Λόγος names both in their reciprocal relation and is thus the word for the primordial conflict between the two. If we lend to the word "logic" a sense befitting this insight, then it is no longer the name for a field of academic philosophy. Logic then names the site where the primordial conflict between thinking and being each time flares up. The name "logic" gains a mighty sound. If we hear it in this way, then let us only note that it can be no accident when the highest peak that Western metaphysics climbs, namely Hegel's *Logic,* bears this name.

Now we suddenly see that even the directive capacity of the chosen signpost reaches a little further than we first presumed. For at first we only looked for a guiding thread which was supposed to supply the answer to the question, briefly put, as to what was meant by the talk of thinking "as such" ["*dem*" *Denken*] in the phrase "Basic Principles of Thinking" [*des Denkens*]. In the meantime, something else came to light which can be stated thus: Thinking is never only "logical" in that it follows the laws of thought, rather there are these laws as basic principles because thinking is from the outset "logical," i.e., is ground-positing [*Grund-setzend*] and so is referred to the ground, i.e., to the Λόγος as the being of beings.

Even if we only broadly examine these connections, we must realize at which place the meditation concerning the basic principles of thinking plays itself out, namely on the field of the Λόγος. This meditation runs through various epochs of the history of Western thinking until it can prepare the play-space determined for it. It is advisable to note this so that we do not take too lightly the transition attempted in the

11. Translator's Note: See the 1951 lecture "Logos (Heraklit, Fragment 50)," first delivered in Bremen and published the same year, now in *Vorträge und Aufsätze,* ed. Friedrich-Wilhelm von Herrmann, *Gesamtausgabe* vol. 7 (Frankfurt am Main: Vittorio Klostermann, 2000), 211–34. English translation: "Logos (Heraclitus, Fragment B 50)," trans. David Farrell Krell, in Martin Heidegger, *Early Greek Thinking,* ed. David Farrell Krell (San Francisco: Harper & Row, 1984), 59–78.

principle of identity from a meditation concerning a basic principle to a discussion of what it posits. Along the path now walked, the transition, assuming it can still be called such, is announced in that we invoke a third kind of equivocality in the talk of "Basic Principles of Thinking." But already the naming of this third "transformation of sense" would like to say that what are now called principles and ground and thinking are to be experienced differently: principle as leap, ground as abyss, and precisely the abyss of thinking, which itself is also otherwise defined in terms of where it leaps to.

We can experience the leap only in leaping, not through utterances about it. But these are able to prepare for the leap if they speak of what it leaps away from, of that wherein it is accordingly bound, in order to reach the space of freedom.

The field for the leap of departure is provided by the tradition. Indeed already early on and all at once we find in shifting form the traces of a meditation upon the basic principles. Indeed it first gets under way expressly and along a secured course with the beginning of modern philosophy, and even here at first only hesitantly, though pointedly.

Only with Leibniz, it must be said here, does the meditation concerning the basic principles arrive at a fundamental soil [*grundsätzlichen Boden*] from which can grow the doctrine of the basic principles in Kant and speculative idealism. Instead of a more detailed presentation, which is not possible here, a preparatory remark may be repeated that Leibniz affixed to one of his short treatises, barely encompassing three pages and without title.[12] The preparatory remark reads: *Cum animadverterem plerosque omnes de principiis meditantes aliorum potius exempla quam*

---

12. G. W. Leibniz, "X. Ohne Überschrift, in Betreff der Mittel der philosophischen Beweisfürhung," in *Die philosophischen Schriften*, ed. C. J. Gerhardt, vol. 7 (Berlin: Weidmann, 1890), 299–301, 299. G. W. Leibniz, "De Principiis Praecipue Contradictionis et Rationis Sufficientis," Nr. 170 in *Sämtliche Schriften und Briefe*, Reihe 6: *Philosophische Schriften*, Band 4: 1677–Juni 1690, Teil A, ed. Leibniz-Forschungsstelle der Universität Münster (Berlin: Akademie Verlag, 1999), 803–806, 804. English translation: G. W. Leibniz, "On the General Characteristic," part 2, in *Philosophical Papers and Letters*, ed. and trans. Leroy E. Loemker, 2nd ed. (Dordrecht: Kluwer Academic Publishers, 1989), 225–27, 225; translation modified.

*rerum naturam sequi, et praejudicia etiam cum id maxime profitentur,
non satis evitare, de meo tentandum aliquid altiusque ordiendum
putavi.* "When I observed that almost all who contemplate principles are sooner to take the conceptions of others as a model
rather than to follow the nature of things, and (thereby) do not
satisfactorily avoid prejudices—even when they greatly proclaim this—I therefore resolved for myself to attempt something on my own and to take a higher and more fundamental
point of departure."

It concerns the point of departure for the *meditare de principiis. Principium,* i.e., *id quod primum capit*—that which grasps and
holds fast and thus holds out before itself that which is first, that
from which something else arises, in that it rests upon the former and is grounded thereupon. Principles are graspings of first
grounds. Precisely these Leibniz wants to contemplate in their
nature and thereby climb higher in the order of meditation.
This means: Leibniz adheres to the order in which being and
thinking, along with the principles that arose here and there,
are both related to one another. Leibniz seeks a deeper founding for this order—from out of the essence of being (*esse*) and
thinking, i.e., from out of the true propositions, the *veritates.*

This says: When Leibniz contemplates the basic principles, he
remains in the sequence and order of the possible steps that are
sketched in advance by the essence of metaphysics and logic. For
him as well as for subsequent thinkers, the meditation upon
basic principles remains of a sort that offers them no impetus and
no occasion capable of directing them to leap away from the field
of the tradition. But where a leap of departure becomes necessary in the contemporary constellation of being and thinking,
this in no way repudiates the tradition. It even brings it more
freely along its way and thereby more tellingly back into its place
of origin. This announces itself to us in that the leap of thinking
arrives at a realm that, in regard to the tradition from which it
leaps away, is the abyss of thinking. In itself, however, this abyss
is that which the earliest beginnings of Western destiny point to,
assuming one succeeds in experiencing them more inceptually.
In so doing we merely follow the signpost a little further back
until it leads to a crossroads.

Lecture V

The meditation of these lectures traverses a path along which we are attempting to situate the phrase "Basic Principles of Thinking." The meditation seeks to indicate the location that the basic principles of thinking reach when we hear this phrase in such a way that it says: leaps[1] of thinking into the abyss, namely into the abyss of thinking. Much rests on knowing what this means: thinking.[2]

As the signpost shows, thinking is our thinking, a thinking indebted to the tradition. As to what it is, this has long been defined by the λόγος. To what extent is an essential relation to the abyss appropriate for a thinking so determined? Answer: insofar as thinking has the character of a founding. The answer sounds nonsensical.

Founding, thought in a Greek manner, means λόγον διδόναι, to give the λόγος, the ground, not only to declare it, but to expose it, to provide it and to yield it: to let the ground, that which underlies, the soil, lie before. Accordingly, thinking as founding is univocally related to the ground and not at all to the abyss.

---

1. on "leap" in the following pages 149–50, cf. Notes to *Identity and Difference*—"Statement" and "Leap." Breaking in—Entrance. Translator's Note: See presumably the supplementary materials to "The Principle of Identity," the "Beilagen zu der Satz der Identität" in *Identität und Differenz*, ed. Friedrich-Wilhelm von Herrmann, *Gesamtausgabe* vol. 11 (Frankfurt am Main: Vittorio Klostermann, 2006), 89–102.

2. ⟨Text variant from the handwritten addenda to the 2nd typescript:⟩ . . . what this means: thinking. We have a signpost that points to the answer. Namely, it is the title "logic" as the name for the doctrine of thinking. As the signpost shows, . . .

Thinking must eschew the latter in the utmost; for the abyss threatens thinking with the collapse of its essence, namely the loss of the possibility for still finding a ground upon which it could ground itself in order to be able to be a founding that would found something.[3] Or so one would like to believe.

But it may finally be the time to ask whether thinking can ever attain its λόγος-like essence of founding as long as it everywhere only remains related to grounds. As long as this occurs, thinking indeed takes its essence, founding, as its measure, but is nonetheless incapable of considering this itself along with its stipulations. If thinking is to consider the relation to ground and the ground as such, it cannot again adhere to a ground; more, it cannot claim to be a founding. Thus thinking must properly reach into the abyss in order to be able to release the essential realm for the ground and our relation to it. If we attend to this more carefully, then the statement that thinking as founding would have an essential relation to the abyss loses its nonsensical character.

At the abyss, thinking finds no more ground. It falls into the bottomless, where nothing bears any longer. But must thinking necessarily be borne? Apparently so, since thinking is no self-mastering activity encapsulated in itself nor a self-propelled toy. Thinking remains from the outset referred to what is to be thought; it is called by this.

Indeed, in any case, must not what does the bearing have the character of a bearer, something that metaphysics represents as a substance or a subject?[4] Not at all. Something like thinking can be borne in that it is suspended. Admittedly, to determine how thinking is able to be suspended, from where this suspension comes to it, all this requires a proper experience and meditation. Both are so idiosyncratic that they probably only thrive from out of the event of appropriation.

Only so long as what is to be thought concernfully approaches us in the character of a ground is thinking, as per the correspondence necessary to it, a founding. How does it come to pass that, for a long time and in regard to everything, it is a

---

3. ⟨Text variant from the handwritten addenda to the 2nd typescript:⟩ . . . , namely the loss of the possibility of still finding something upon which it could ground something else and thereby found.

4. "Bearing" in the sense of granting—owning

ground that provides the measure for thinking of any kind as well as for its procedure?

The signpost had pointed us to where we could expect the answer to this question. At the dawn of Greek thinking, the explanation for why what lies before lies before, why what presences presences, why the being is, was determined as Λόγος. So says Heraclitus. We simply have to acknowledge this, not as an authoritative proclamation, but indeed as a word that our thinking must ever again thoughtfully remember and examine. What does "examine" mean? For even today it still sounds startling, assuming we shake off what is familiar, when the being of beings is defined as the Λόγος. Yet this determination, being as Λόγος, belongs at the same time in the nearest neighborliness to that experience of being that Parmenides perceives in being when he thinks it as the Ἕν, the simple unifying singular unity.

Through an inapparent harmony, the uniting one-all and the Λόγος as gathering in the sense of the Ἕν Πάντα each belong in the same. This same is what is first, from where the being as such is each time a being (being [*Sein*]? presence). Both the Ἕν and the Λόγος still speak, and with a new decisiveness, from out of the unity of dialectical mediation. As this unity, being conditions all beings, grounding them, and as the unconditioned, being is the system of the absolute itself. The "first from whence," τὸ πρῶτον ὅθεν, is called ἀρχή—as the Λόγος, it is the ground that grounds. Neither Heraclitus nor any of the great thinkers say anything sensational, but instead say what is simple of the inexhaustibly same. Therefore we are first ripe for thinking when we have lost our taste for the sensational.

The being of beings is lit up with the character of the λόγος, i.e., of ground. Thus a principle of the kind like the principle of identity, which says that to the being of every being there would belong: itself the same as itself, such a principle is called in an exceptional sense a grounding-principle.

If now the thinking that is defined by λόγος sees itself as posed before the task of contemplating for its own assurance the basic principles that set the standard for it, then for a thinking understood as a founding this can only happen in such a way that it leads even the basic principles back to a first and ultimate ground. The thinking that is stamped by λόγος, defined as founding, thus cannot even come into the danger of reaching an abyss. Everywhere it sees and finds only grounds upon which and with which it calculates. The gigantic contemporary deployment of calculation in technology, industry, economy, and politics attests to the power of a thinking obsessed with the λόγος of logic in a form almost bordering on insanity. The full vehemence of calculative thinking concentrates itself in the centuries of modernity. At its beginning, particularly with Leibniz, the systematic *meditatio de principiis* is also inaugurated.

With this remark we establish an incident merely historiologically within the succession of details in science and in thinking. But if we instead think what is historiologically established here in a historical manner, then we would have to say: The systematic *meditatio de principiis* first casts metaphysics anew and thus opens the historical course of modernity [*der Neuzeit*].

With this state of affairs, a widespread opinion is obliged to make reference to the fact that the new position and formation of mathematics within scientific research have led above all to the explicit contemplation of rules, laws, methods, and axioms, and to their painstaking construction. One can here bring in the text of Descartes that bears the telling title: *Regulae ad directionem ingenii*, or *Rules for the Direction of the Spirit of Invention*.[5] In fact, even if the connections are not clear as day, the text is a foundational book of modern technological thinking, which itself is at the same time mathematical thinking. For a long time now, the framing of axioms has belonged to Western mathematics. Yet mathematics contemplates the principles not because it is mathematics, but rather because Greek mathematics in an exceptional sense remains in accord with the λόγος- and ἀρχή-character of thinking. If we attend to this then even the judgment just mentioned about the role of mathematics and its significance for metaphysical thinking is straightened out. We must ask: Why is it that in modernity

---

5. Translator's Note: René Descartes, *Regulae ad directionem ingenii*, in *Oeuvres de Descartes*, 11 vols., eds. Charles Adam and Paul Tannery (Paris: Librairie Philosophique J. Vrin, 1966), vol. 10, 359–469. English translation: *Rules for the Direction of the Mind*, in *The Philosophical Writings of Descartes*, 3 vols., ed. John Cottingham, Robert Stoothoff, and Dugald Murdoch (Cambridge: Cambridge University Press, 1985), vol. 1, 7–78.

mathematics is newly developed into an authoritative form of thinking? By no means merely in the fecundity of mathematics as a methodological instrument, also not in that, since long ago and once again, measure, number, and figures become the "key to all creatures."[6] The mathematical finds such a decisive entry into modern metaphysics because within this metaphysics itself something essential has been decided for it: namely, the alteration of the essence of truth into certainty. This alteration determines the truth[7] as a self-knowing, i.e., self-grounding, founding of all that is knowable from the unity of an unconditioned[8] ground. This alteration of the essence of truth, which we only coarsely indicate by what has been said, is no consequence of the influence of the mathematical way of thinking; rather that essential alteration of truth first opened up the metaphysical play-space for mathematics to thoroughly dominate modern science in a particular direction. What its own axioms and principles are according to their essence, mathematics itself can neither say nor even ask. That today attempts in this direction are nonetheless undertaken within mathematics and mathematical logic and are taken for authoritative, i.e., adequate in principle, throws a light on the genuine historical processes of our age. They effect an increasing blindness in regard to the basic principles of thinking and their essential provenance because they hold the λóγος-character of thinking, and this in its modern mathematicized form, for unconditional and as solely authoritative.

The decisive impetus to a transformation of logic, something that today is in full stride, stems in the same way as the

---

6. Translator's Note: "When numerals and figures are no longer / the key to all creatures . . ." from Novalis, Paralipomena to *Heinrich von Ofterdingen,* "Die Berliner Papiere," in Novalis, *Schriften: Die Werke Friedrich von Hardenbergs,* vol. 1: *Das dichterische Werk,* ed. Paul Kluckhohn and Richard Samuel with Heinz Ritter and Gerhard Schulz (Stuttgart: W. Kohlhammer Verlag, 1960), 340–48, 344.

7. ⟨Text variant from the handwritten addenda to the 2nd typescript:⟩ This unfolds itself . . .

8. The ground is unconditioned insofar as it itself for itself is the ground of itself and requires no other ground than this. (In which way does "identity" essence in the unity of the unconditioned ground?)

meditatio de principiis from the thinking of Leibniz. As a result of this transformation, logic as mathematical logic and logistics has an essential share in the steering of the modern technological world. Here let us briefly note: The signpost does not only point backwards into the provenance of thinking from out of the λόγος, it also points ahead into the most extreme implementation of calculative thinking and the increasing reification of its dominance.

The signpost bears the name "logic." It points us along the path that lets be known: Thinking is determined by the λόγος. Pointing further, the signpost shows: Logic unveils itself now as the name for the meditation upon the λόγος, as the site of the primordial conflict between thinking and being. Pointing further still, the signpost, as mentioned, should lead us to a crossroads.

This is a place where the path along which our meditation concerning the essential provenance of thinking is already proceeding, is crossed [*durchquert*] by another one. To go cross-country [*querfeldein*] means to cut through the fields. Another path cuts across our path hitherto. We would have already noticed that something of this sort could befall our path, had we followed attentively enough the first characterization of the course of the discussion.

At first it was stated that the task was to clarify the equivocality of the phrase "Basic Principles of Thinking." Three kinds of equivocality were enumerated: 1. The double meaning of the genitive; 2. The ambiguity of the talk of "the" thinking; 3. An alteration of sense.

One easily sees: What is named in the third place, strictly thought, is no longer even a kind of equivocality, but rather something completely different, which pertains to the phrase "Basic Principles of Thinking" as a whole and, so to speak, cuts across the previously mentioned double meaning and ambiguity. For according to the alteration of sense, "principle" no longer means a setting together in the sense of the λόγος ἀποφαντικός, but rather "leap." "Ground" is understood, thoroughly askew [*verquer*] but necessarily, as "abyss," because the essence of the ground itself can no longer be a ground, but rather must be such that the determination "ground" is kept at bay. Grounding-principles now mean leaps into the abyss, and indeed leaps of thinking precisely into the abyss of thinking.

Thinking leaps away from ground, i.e., from the character of founding as what was hitherto the sole standard, away from ground as being, which for all founding-calculating representation of beings remains what is to be thought and likewise what is always already thought. Thinking leaps away from thinking and being, away from the λόγος-based definition that occasions the primordial conflict between the two, which Heraclitus already names by the single word Λόγος, a Λόγος which, as the Ἕν Πάντα, is also called Ἔρις: conflict. Through this leap of departure, thinking does not leave the primordial conflict behind it unresolved, rather it takes it along with it, so to speak, in order to inceptually [*an-fänglich*] experience the plainness of the belonging together of thinking and being. Accordingly, thinking looks out to whether and how in the leap it would open the realm wherein sameness itself essences.

Thus by its leaping into the abyss, thinking relinquishes its λόγος-character in a certain way and nonetheless does not forget that from the outset it would be determined by the Λόγος. For it was indeed said that the signpost that would point from the λόγος into the place of origin would point still further back, beyond the primordial conflict, to a crossroads. Here the course along the path hitherto comes to a standstill and thereby the Λόγος is first wholly brought into view, i.e., in terms of the whole of its essential place of origin, if otherwise the course must keep to the crossroads.

And, in fact, it does come to such a standstill. What lies, so to speak, askew [*quer*]? This, that λόγος originarily[9] is neither the word for thinking nor even the word for being. Instead, early on with the Greeks, λόγος is the word for talk and λέγειν the word for talking. In view of this λόγος that here cuts across our path, we ask: What does talking mean, what do the Greeks see as the basic trait of talk in that they understand talking as λέγειν? For from early on and just as indisputably, λέγειν means so much as gathering, bringing together, and letting what is brought in lie before, bringing-before. Philology stubbornly proclaims: λόγος "authentically" means talk. This proclamation is correct to the same degree that it remains a half-measure. For

---

9. ⟨Text variant from the handwritten addenda to the 2nd typescript:⟩ inceptually (instead of: originarily)

us, talk and talking customarily belong in the horizon of what is known as speech and speaking. With this assignment of talk to speech, we act as though we knew what speech meant and in what its essence lies. But we are far removed from this knowledge. For this reason we use the word "speech" with all reservations. For it could be that talk and talking and the corresponding λόγος and λέγειν can never be defined by speaking and by speech. This is also, in fact, the case. Already our own speech, whose treasures we scarcely know any longer, clearly attests that talk does not genuinely mean that which we conceive as speech. Still in Middle High German and even earlier, talk rightly meant univocally that which we also still mean when we say: to give someone a talking to, to demand an account, i.e., information, about something, that this person should bring forth what lies before.

Talk and talking do not mean speaking and speech in the sense of an uttering of expressions; talk means precisely that which from early on λέγειν, λόγος means: bringing before, bringing collectively to appearance. The most beautiful testament for this sense of talk and λόγος is at the same time the oldest, which the tradition keeps ready for us. It[10] is found in Homer's *Odyssey*, first book, verse 56. In all of Homer's work, the word λόγος only appears in this place and indeed in the plural with two adjectives in the turn of phrase: μαλακοὶ καὶ αἱμύλιοι λόγοι, "mild and charming speech."[11] Αἱμύλιος means charming, captivating, enchanting. The λόγος can have this trait only insofar as it lets something appear which it gathers to itself, draws to itself. To draw is to pull out. He pulls out, suddenly draws, the sword. This sudden drawing [*Ziehende*] to itself is a pulling out [*Entzückende*], a carrying away [*Entrück-ende*], and therefore something charming [*Berückende*]. Only insofar as the λόγος by its essence lets something shine forth

10. ⟨Text variant from the handwritten addenda to the 2nd typescript:⟩ The word λόγος

11. Homer, *Homeri Opera*, Scriptorum classicorum Bibliotheca Oxoniensis (Oxford / New York: Clarendon Press / Humphrey Milford, n.d.), line 56. Homer, *Homeri Opera*, vol. 3: *Odysseae Libros I–XII Continens*, ed. Thomas W. Allen (Oxford: Oxford University Press, 1950), line 56. English translation: "with soft and flattering words," Homer, *The Odyssey of Homer*, trans. Richmond Lattimore (New York: HarperPerennial, 1999), 28.

and appear, and in this sense playfully solicits and conjures, can it also occasionally enchant and bewitch, which is nothing other than an exceptional way of gathering, that is, of λέγειν. Thus λόγος and λέγειν authentically, and from early on, do not mean talk and talking in the sense of speaking—but rather? In our language we have only one fitting word for this and it is "saying" [*sagen*]. A basic characteristic of saying is the gathering letting appear. Every speaking and talking and writing is a way of saying, but saying is not necessarily a speaking in the sense of a utilization of speech organs.

Μαλακός and αἰμύλιος, "mild and charming," are not traits of the λόγοι as talking in the sense of speaking; they do not pertain to something vocalized, rather they pertain to the λόγος as saying, one that lets appear and only thereby can charm and captivate.[12]

What do we experience at the crossroads through this insight into the earliest attestation of λόγος? This: The λόγος reigns as saying in the sense of a letting appear and bringing forth.

Saying is a bringing as a bringing-to, which at the same time brings us away from here and brings us into what is said. The gentle power [*Gewalt*] of a bringing pervades saying. From here on we first recognize to what extent λόγος could become the determining character of thinking.

Thinking is[13] νοεῖν, perceiving [*vernehmen*]: putting forth and taking up [*vor- und aufnehmen*], i.e., gathering, bringing to the fore that which presences in its presencing. Because λόγος is in essence a saying (bringing), it could also be cast in that basic form of thinking that we know as the utterance, the proposition, and that we recognize in logic as the sole standard. Indeed, the utterance in the sense of ἀπόφανσις is only one way of saying, namely one that brings what is present to appearance and establishes it in appearance in this or that outward appearance.

Every utterance is a saying. But not every saying is necessarily an utterance in the sense of a logical proposition. Therefore the λόγος as utterance can never be taken as the guiding thread for a meditation that pursues the essence of saying. Saying,

12. λόγοι—does not first or even only mean the "vocalization" of talk; this itself has its character invariably from the manner of saying.

13. ⟨Text variant from the handwritten addenda to the 2nd typescript:⟩ (since Parmenides)

however, as the bringing just characterized, is also never merely the belated linguistic expression of thinking, but rather thinking is from the outset a saying, presumably the inceptual saying, pervading all ways of saying. Here we encounter the decisive hint for the attempt to speak of language and its essence. If the talk is of language, we now mean its essence as determined by saying, by the inceptually experienced λόγος.

Thinking as saying is related to the presencing of what presences, to being. As previously mentioned, the house of being is language, this now thought from its essence that conceals itself in saying.[14] Being and thinking, the primordial conflict of the two, is native to language, whose essence resounds in Λόγος and is to be considered in respect to saying.

It belongs to the secrets of the dispensation under which the thinking of the Greeks stood, that so early on the essence of language resounded as λόγος and that this resounding nevertheless was not perceived as such and properly considered, but rather just as soon faded away. Instead of this, the Greek observation of language struck out in a direction that, with manifold variations, has remained the standard until today for all scientific research into language and philosophical interpretation of the essence of language. It is the conception of language defined from φωνή, from vocalization, and from the γλῶσσα, the tongue, *lingua*, the phonetic-linguistic representation. The metalinguistic treatment of language that is now coming to predominance in the Anglo-Saxon countries, the production of "metalanguages," is surely not the liberation from linguistics, but rather its perfect reification, just as metaphysics is the perfection of physics.

The essence of language, according to the conventional conception, is neither thought from the inceptually experienced λόγος nor is the essence of the λόγος itself brought into the space of freedom, much rather the λόγος is forced into the narrowed perspective of "logic," which for its part lends its stamp to grammar as the doctrine of language in the sense of linguistics.

And now we read the signpost completely for the first time, yet differently once again. Logic is not only the doctrine of thinking. Logic is not only the site for the primordial conflict between thinking and being. Logic is—now thought from

---

14. Translator's Note: see GA 79: 128/120.

λόγος as saying and this experienced as the essential resonance of language—logic is the soliloquy [*Selbstgespräch*] of language with its essence.[15]

The abyss into which thinking leaps is the essence of language. This essence conceals itself in the essence of saying. Through its leaping, thinking alters itself, insofar as it more inceptually enters into its essence as saying. At the same time as this, the talk of "essence" receives a correspondingly transformed sense.

Now it does not require a copious amount of evidence to see that with every attempt to leap into the essence of language we instantly find ourselves pressured on all sides by conceptions, perspectives, and questions that remain standard for all previous treatments of language and have become established customs. These were already mentioned. They cannot be further surveyed or fruitfully arranged unless, with a little violence, one were to lead them back to a few guiding horizons, a business that does not belong in the course of this lecture.

In the meantime, because every leap remains a leap of departure from the tradition, and this itself is at the same time invariably richer in hidden gifts than a mere quest for novelty would like to believe, we cannot so easily turn ourselves away from the customary conceptions of language. We ourselves cannot do this, even if these conceptions occasionally so mislead our meditation into the essence of language that we only later see through this.

Where something is so beset in the way the essence of language is, the preparation of the leap is indeed necessarily elaborate, even more elaborate, assuming this comparison is allowed, than the most beautiful dialogues of Plato, which, as one can establish, in their to-and-fro and back-and-forth of saying and questioning are precisely without results for the one who goes hunting for utterances and a doctrine instead of hearing what is unsaid in the saying of the conversation. The uninitiated believe that the unsaid is only the remainder that remains lying behind what is said. Indeed the unsaid has its place only in

---

15. To what extent a conversation [*Gespräch*]? To what extent a self-conversation [*Selbst-Gespräch*]? What does it mean: with its essence?

what is said and only through the highest force of saying can it become and be such. Through the unsaid we first catch sight of the *issue* of thinking in its whole importance.

To achieve a first view into this space of freedom, in order to sharpen the glance into the essence of language already attempted, we restrict ourselves to a single state of affairs. It already became visible at the crossroads where the λόγος as thinking, in the sense of the λόγος ἀποφαντικός, and the λόγος as talk, in the sense of saying, encounter each other. If we put this into a formula, then it concerns the relationship between thinking and language. The negotiations around this topic find no end, because they lack the right beginning. What is missing? The insight that thinking cannot be discussed in isolation on its own; for without a look to the relation of thinking to being we always have merely a fragment of the essence of thinking before us. If we indeed make the relation of language and thinking into a theme, then we must direct our meditation to the relationship between *thinking* and *being* and *language*. Then there appears at a stroke the whole quandary our enterprise has gotten itself into. For obviously *thinking, being,* and *language* cannot be placed together like three things. The relationship between thinking, being, and language never first arises in that we weave together the reciprocal relations between the three. The relationship that they hold to each other is rather something still unexperienced in which the belonging together of thinking, being, and language resonates. We still lack the view for this relationship, but also the ear for what the word here says. Nevertheless, we seek assistance to bring the relationship of these three into view and in so doing find out that we ourselves belong in this relationship in that we, as needed in the relationship, dwell in it and build on it. The relationship of thinking, being, and language therefore does not lie over against us. We ourselves are held within it. We can neither overtake it, nor even merely catch up with it, because we ourselves are caught up in this relationship. On this we would like to note that the elaborateness and awkwardness that our contemplation must go through do not merely stem from the limitations of our capacities, but instead are essential. This gives no right to whine about the wretchedness of the human, but is instead a cause for jubilation over the plenitude of the riddle that remains preserved for thinking.

But now how does the relationship between thinking, being, and language, in which we belong as the thinkers, join these together? We are not to lose sight of what the signpost ultimately revealed. Formally, it can be put so: Being and thinking, they themselves in their belonging together, are transposed back upon the λόγος as saying and thus back upon language. Language shows itself as the ground, thinking and being as its appearances. Thinking and being are grounded in language. It gives the relation its hold.[16]

Indeed, when we present the state of affairs in this way, do we not fall back into the conception of ground and grounding, now when we are supposed to be residing in the region of the abyss? But even if for the moment we are not disturbed by this falling back, we will nevertheless oppose the suggestion that we conceive language as the ground for being and thinking.

Language, whether conceived as speaking or talking or saying, is an activity of the human. Can being ever be explained as a production of the human? Evidently not. This is sooner the case for thinking, insofar as the human thinks because he speaks. Or does he speak because he thinks? Or do neither of these adequately hold? In the meantime, another way is proffered to concede an exceptional role to language in the whole of the relationship between thinking, being, and language. When one conceives language as the expression of something and as a sign for something, then it emerges that being is language, insofar as being is spoken through language. Thinking is language, insofar as it is expressed in speaking. For a long time now, and not without basis, one has used the representation of signs as an aid for conceiving what is linguistic of language. For this reason, we can by no means take lightly this long-established respect in which language becomes visible almost as of its own accord right when one asks what it would

_____

16. Cf. now "Kant's Thesis about Being" (1961) (Frankfurt am Main: Vittorio Klostermann, 1963), 32ff. ⟨Martin Heidegger, *Wegmarken*, ed. Friedrich-Wilhelm von Herrmann, *Gesamtausgabe* vol. 9 (Frankfurt am Main: Vittorio Klostermann, 1976), 445–80, 475–80. English translation: "Kant's Thesis about Being," trans. Ted E. Klein Jr. and William E. Pohl, rev. trans. William McNeill in *Pathmarks*, ed. William McNeill (Cambridge: Cambridge University Press, 1998), 337–63, 359–63.⟩ Translator's Note: this is a marginal note in the German text (see above, xv).

be. Not even when we have acknowledged that this respect, which represents language to us as expression, remains the most ensnaring obstruction for an *entrance* [Einkehr][17] into the essence of language.

But now it is worth noting that this sweeping accomplishment, which certainly pertains to language as expression for being and thinking, nonetheless does not hit upon what is thought when we say: The essence of language is what does the holding in the relationship that holds being and thinking to each other in their belonging together. This utterance, if it is one, retains its bewildering character. We are sooner inclined to arrange the relationship just named otherwise and say: Language and thinking are grounded in being; for while both are something extant, being has the character of ground. Language and thinking are grounded in being, without this they would be nothing.

Indeed, in the same instant we are also reminded: Being as ground determines thinking as a founding. This relation between ground and founding stems from the primordial conflict of Λόγος. But according to the directive of the signpost that reaches furthest back, the Λόγος is a talking, saying. Accordingly there reigns in the primordial conflict of the Λόγος, as what is genuinely contentious, the λόγος in the sense of saying. However dark and foreign to us the relation between language, thinking, and being may appear, it reveals a cast and trait that we have to face if we do not want to high-handedly disregard the signpost and its directing ability.

If we take a more sustained look into what is indicated there, then it cannot escape us that the λόγος does not appear there as language in the sense of a speaking vocalization, as expression. The λόγος is a saying in the sense of a letting appear. We must[18] discuss language in regard to saying when we search for its essence and should no longer elucidate and explain it as a speech activity.

The discussion now necessary harbors within it the leap of thinking into its abyss—into the essence of language. Here "essence" no longer means ground of possibility, no longer

---

17. and thus not "leap"!

18. ⟨Text variant from the handwritten addenda to the 2nd typescript:⟩ Where does this "must" come from?

essentia, essentiality as the highest species, no longer the τὸ τί ἦν εἶναι of Aristotle, no longer "essence" in the sense of Hegel's logic. Essence is a persevering as a granting and this an appropriating [*das Ereignen*]. The essencing of language as saying is the realm [*Be-reich*]. This word is here claimed as a *singulare tantum.* It names something singular, that wherein all things and beings extend to one another [*zu-gereicht*], reach over [*überreicht*], and thus reach [*erreichen*] one another, and redound [*gereichen*] to the benefit and detriment of each other, fulfill [*ausreichen*] and satisfy one another.[19]

This[20] realm alone is likewise home to the unattainable [*das Unerreichbare*]. The realm, now to be experienced as the essencing of language, is the dominion [*Reich*] of play, wherein all relationships of things and beings playfully solicit each other and mirror each other. Saying is reaching in the sense of the realm [*des Be-reichs*]. The reference to this only allows us to distantly intimate the essence of language as saying. The realm is the location in which thinking and being belong together.

The location is itself the relationship of the two. This relationship was earlier indicated by the phrase: Language is the house of being.[21] "House" here means precisely what the word says: protection, guardianship, container [*Be-hältnis*], relationship [*Ver-hältnis*]. In the talk of the house of being, "being" means being itself.[22] But this means precisely the belonging together with thinking, the *belonging*-together that first determines being as being. In the phrase just cited, "language" is not conceived as speaking and thus not as a mere activity of the human, but rather as house, i.e., as protection, as relationship.

The relationship is repeatedly pointed to by another citation, which says: Language speaks and not the human.[23] The human speaks only insofar as he corresponds to language.

---

19. ⟨Text variant from the handwritten addenda to the 2nd typescript:⟩ What extends-toward [*Das Zu-reichende*], "reaching-forth" [*Hinreichende*], to enrich [*Er-reichern*] (to increase).

20. ⟨Text variant from the handwritten addenda to the 2nd typescript:⟩ thought in such a manner

21. Translator's Note: see above, GA 79: 128/120, 162/153.

22. and the ontological difference

23. Translator's Note: see Heidegger's 1955–56 Freiburg lecture series *Der Satz vom Grund,* ed. Petra Jaeger, *Gesamtausgabe* vol. 10 (Frankfurt am

Language speaks. At first, this sounds like a tautology, outside of which one cannot conceive how language is supposed
to speak, since indeed it itself is not equipped with speech
organs. What proffers itself as a tautology, however, i.e., that
language speaks, is the indication that the essence of language
itself is playful, though it thereby does not get tangled up in
itself, but releases itself into the free space of that inceptual
freedom that is determined by itself alone.

We come closer to this state of affairs by contemplating the
realm as the relationship which holds open the belonging together of thinking and being. Indeed, in the words "language
speaks" what does this "speaks" mean if it cannot mean "speaking" in the sense of the activity of speech organs?

Language speaks as pronouncement [*Spruch*], as appeal [*Zu-
spruch*], and as claim [*Anspruch*]. Language is so playful that
speaking, as in this case, means the same as saying. Otherwise
linguistic doctrine teaches something else in explaining that
the verbs "to speak" and "to talk" can be used absolutely [in-
transitively], in distinction from the verb "to say." In saying
there constantly lies a relation to something to be said and to
what is said. Saying is relative to that [transitive]. If we consider
more closely the sense of the verbs "to speak," "to talk," "to
say," then we must surely emphasize against linguistic doctrine
that ever only in saying does the whole essence of language
come to appearance, and in this sense absolutely so. Only externally, grammatically represented, are speaking and talking
used absolutely [intransitively], i.e., here: separated and cut off
from the whole essence of language.

One speaks. Someone talks. . . . He rattles on perhaps because he has nothing to say. And one speaks endlessly and it
all says nothing. Contrariwise, one can be silent and in such a
way say much, while there is no silence that speaks. Even the
speechless gesture, precisely this, resonates in saying, not because there is a language of gestures and forms, but because
the essence of language lies in saying. Gestures are not at first
mere gestures that subsequently express something and then

Main: Vittorio Klostermann, 1997), 143. English translation: *The Principle of Reason*, trans. Reginald Lily (Bloomington: Indiana University
Press, 1991), 96.

become a language, rather gestures are in themselves what they are through saying, wherein their bearing, enduring, and conveying each time remain already gathered. Gestural bearing is determined by saying and is thereby constantly the resonance of restraint. The gestural first attunes all movements. The nonessence of the gesture is the gesticulation. Pure gestures are speechless, but they are not wordless. They are so little this that they constantly are achieved[24] in terms of and through such a saying. The nonspeaking essence of language resonates in saying. Saying constantly says something and only thereby from time to time also says nothing. Saying something is invariably and simultaneously a saying to a hearing. Language speaks from out of a saying. The essence of language is the saying [*die Sage*]. We use this word "saying" now—like many words of our language—mostly in a disparaging sense: saying as mere saying, something not confirmed and thereby unbelievable. Saying is not so meant here, if this word is to hint at the essence of language. It is meant more in the sense of legend, which as fable [*Mär*] is connected with the fairy tale [*Märchen*]. The essence of language is presumably the genuinely fabulous [*Märchenhafte*].

We humans can only say insofar as we are already accorded, promised, to the essence of language as saying. Indeed what does "saying" authentically mean? We attain a first answer by listening to what the Greek λέγειν and λόγος say: appearing—and letting appear—conjuring. The same is meant by our[25] word *sagan*; it means to show, to point, to see—and to let be perceived. Saying is a disclosive-concealing showing and pointing, a so-defined extending toward . . . , and a reaching back and forth. Saying is the realm [*Be-reich*] of this hinting-showing reaching.

Showing, according to its original[26] essence, precisely does not have need of signs, i.e., showing is not merely the use of signs, but rather showing as letting appear first makes possible

---

24. ⟨Text variant from the handwritten addenda to the 2nd typescript:⟩ complete their reach.

25. ⟨Text variant from the handwritten addenda to the 2nd typescript:⟩ German

26. ⟨Text variant from the handwritten addenda to the 2nd typescript:⟩ ownmost (instead of: original)

the institution and use[27] of signs. Only because language is in its essence saying, a showing in the original sense,[28] are there vocal signs and written signs for talking and speaking. Only because language is in its essence saying and as such shows, can this showing become a letting be seen of views and points of view, which we name images and which writing evokes not only as phonetic writing, but also as pictographic writing.[29]

Only through an adequate discussion of saying can we understand the original λόγος-character of thinking. Thinking is in its essence saying. Poetizing is singing. Every singing is a saying, but not every saying a singing.

The etymology of "saying" goes back to the Indo-Germanic *sequ*, which recurs in the Greek ἐπ—ἔπος—ἔνεπε and is to be heard in the first verse of Homer's *Odyssey*: Ἄνδρα μοι ἔννεπε, Μοῦσα, πολύτροπον;[30] "Say to me of that man, muse, the one much driven about." The muse sings in that she says and addresses the saying to the singer. So construed, then, song and thought, the collection of singing and of thinking respectively, are both at home in the same essence, in what is legendary of the saying [*Sagenhaften der Sage*]. Thus, for example, Antigone and Oedipus and Tiresias in the dramas of Sophocles have not spoken as psychologically trained speakers, instead they have said and thereby have sung. In saying they let appear what they have caught sight of, namely that which has sighted them themselves.

From the foregoing discussion, thoughts about language that we heard from the German Classic and Romantic period become understandable, for example, the saying of Johann

---

27. ⟨Text variant from the handwritten addenda to the 2nd typescript:⟩ application (instead of: use)

28. ⟨Text variant from the handwritten addenda to the 2nd typescript:⟩ the world-indicating showing (instead of: in the original sense of showing)

29. The essence of the image from out of "belonging" [*Gehörig*].

30. Homer, *Homeri Opera*, Scriptorum classicorum Bibliotheca Oxoniensis (Oxford / New York: Clarendon Press / Humphrey Milford, n.d.), line 1. Homer, *Homeri Opera*, vol. 3: *Odysseae Libros I–XII Continens*, ed. Thomas W. Allen (Oxford: Oxford University Press, 1950), line 1. English translation: "Tell me, Muse, of the man of many ways"; Homer, *The Odyssey of Homer*, trans. Richmond Lattimore (New York: HarperPerennial, 1999), 27.

Georg Hamann: "Poesy is the mother-tongue of the human race."[31] Accordingly the essence of language would have to be understood from the essence of poetry. Such was said in the lecture "Hölderlin and the Essence of Poetry" from 1936.[32] But from where is the essence of poetry to be thought? From what is legendary of the realm that first gives thinking and poetizing over to their respective essences.

Thus we would have to think that saying of Hölderlin which hints at a great deal, "Poetically dwells / the human on this earth," still more deeply by a leap in order to make it wholly our own. The human dwells poetically because he is legendarily accorded [*sagenhaft . . . zugesagt*] to the essence of language as saying [*der Sage*].

We do not come near to the relationship that holds poetizing and thinking apart and together as long as we stretch it across the rack of the relationship between poesy and philosophy.

Grounding-principles of thinking are leaps into the essence of language, which we name "saying." What is legendary of them is that manifold reaching as which the realm resonates in itself. The realm is the location of the identity of thinking and being.

Thinking is saying, but not necessarily talking and speaking and writing. Thinking is saying, but not necessarily utterance in the sense of the λόγος ἀποφαντικός of logic, not necessarily a talking through in the sense of λέγειν as the διαλέγεσθαι of dialectic.

Admittedly, we have very little to say of the essence of saying and its legendary character. We would first have to experience

---

31. Johann Georg Hamann, *"Aesthetica in nuce,"* in *Sämtliche Werke,* historisch-kritische Ausgabe von Josef Nadler, vol. 2: *Schriften über Philosophie/Philologie/Kritik* 1758–1763 (Vienna: Verlag Herder, 1950), 195–217, 197. English translation: Johann Georg Hamann, "Aesthetica in nuce," in *Writings on Philosophy and Language,* ed. and trans. Kenneth Haynes (Cambridge: Cambridge University Press, 2007), 60–95, 63; translation modified.

32. Martin Heidegger, "Hölderlin und das Wesen der Dichtung" (1936). GA 4, pp. 33–48. English translation: "Hölderlin and the Essence of Poetry" in *Elucidations of Hölderlin's Poetry,* trans. Keith Hoeller (Amherst, N.Y.: Humanity Books, 2000), 51–65.

and withstand what is most bewildering: That before all being and thinking, and before the *belonging*-together of both of these, the essence of language is the play of the location, resonating in itself, for this belonging-together. As such a realm [*Bereich*], the saying hands over [*überreicht*] all things and beings to one another and thus extends [*darreicht*] them to us such that we everywhere encounter [*erreichen*] them or miss them.

But it would indeed be even more bewildering if what was bewildering of the legendary realm—language's essence, playful in itself—had flashed up here and there and, in the interim, we did not learn—on long paths to be sure—to occasionally catch sight of the afterglow of such flashes. The testimonial of one such flash may be cited in conclusion. The title reads "Monologue"; the text runs:

> There is really something very foolish about speaking and writing; proper conversation is merely a word game. One can only marvel at the ridiculous mistake that people make when they think—that they speak for the sake of things. The particular quality of language, the fact that it is concerned only with itself, is known to no one. Language is such a marvelous and fruitful secret—because when someone speaks merely for the sake of speaking, he utters the most splendid, most original truths. But if he wants to speak about something definite, capricious language makes him say the most ridiculous and confused stuff. This is also the cause of the hatred that so many serious people feel toward language. They notice the mischief ⟨i.e. the inclination of language to wantonness⟩, but not the fact that the chattering they scorn is the infinitely serious aspect of language. If one could only make people understand that it is the same with language as with mathematical formulae. These constitute a world of their own. They play only with themselves, express nothing but their own marvelous nature, and just for this reason they are so expressive—just for this reason the strange play of relations between things is mirrored in them. Only through their freedom are they elements of nature and only in their free movements does the world-soul manifest itself in them and make them a sensitive

measure and ground plan of things. So it is with language, too—
on the one hand, anyone who is sensitive to its fingering, its
rhythm, its musical spirit, who perceives within himself the deli-
cate working of its inner nature, and moves his tongue or his
hand accordingly, will be a prophet; on the other hand, anyone
who knows how to write truths like these but does not have ear
and sense enough for it will be outwitted by language itself and
mocked by people as Cassandra was by the Trojans. Even if in
saying this I believe I have described the essence and office of
poesy in the clearest possible way, at the same time I know that
no one can understand it, and I have said something quite foolish
because I wanted to say it, and in this way no poesy comes about.
What would it be like though if I had to speak? and this instinct
of language to speak were the hallmark of what inspires language, of the efficacy of language within me? and were my will to
want only everything that I was obliged to do, in the end could
this be poesy without my knowledge or belief and could it make
a secret of language understandable? and thus I would be a born
writer, for a writer is surely only a language enthusiast?

The testimonial stems from Friedrich von Hardenberg (Novalis); it is the sketch of a contribution for the *Athenäum* and was
written in 1799–1800.[33] Much remains dark and confusing in
this monologue of λόγος, especially since he thinks in another
direction and speaks in another language than what is attempted in these lectures.

In the meantime, the consideration has certainly already
established itself that here language, or indeed its essence,
would be made absolute. So it appears in fact as long as we,
insisting on representation, take the essence of language for
something present-at-hand and pre-given, instead of leaping

33. Novalis, "Monolog," in *Briefe und Werke*, vol. 3, ed. Ewald Wasmuth (Berlin: Lambert Schneider Verlag, 1943), 11–12. Novalis, "Monolog," in *Novalis, Schriften: Die Werke Friedrich von Hardenbergs*, vol. 2: *Das
philosophische Werk I*, ed. Richard Samuel with Hans-Joachim Mähl and
Gerhard Schulz (Stuttgart: W. Kohlhammer Verlag, 1965), 672–73. English translation: Novalis, "Monologue," in *Philosophical Writings*, ed. and
trans. Margaret Mahony Stoljar (Albany: State University of New York
Press, 1997), 83–84; translation modified.

into that relationship[34] that the saying *is* as the realm, a relationship in which we ourselves are included.

A look to this, however, charges our thinking with once again examining whether the states of affairs named by the words "relationship," "realm," "saying," "event of appropriation" are still to be represented by concepts. A meditation is roused as to whether a thinking is not required whose language would correspond to the essence of the saying and the saying of essence and therefore would not be able to make use of modified metaphysical terminology. This other thinking must listen back into the unspent vocabulary of our language wherein an unused saying waits in order to help the thinking of what is unthought come into words. Yet this vocabulary by itself can never take away from thinking the risk of its path.

Thinking, however, does not deliver itself over to language, but situates the essence of language in the essential provenance of saying, that relationship within which we are included.

We remain settled upon this earth in relationality. Someone who is only concerned with being right, instead of with the experience of the issue and its claim, could counter to this: Then the relational is precisely the absolute. Correct. But the question surely remains whether we get along in thinking with what is merely correct and with the help of what is correct can ever say what this would then mean: absolute.

For now, another consideration weighs more heavily. When we say: The abyss of thinking is the essence of language. Its essence is the saying. The saying is the realm of the hinting-showing reaching. The realm *is* as the location of the belonging together of thinking and being—when we say this, it appears as though we only followed a chain of utterances. What so appears and can even be taken exclusively in this way every time is nevertheless simultaneously a hint into a saying that encircles itself and thereby directly remains open, just like a ring, which as a ring is indeed closed, but precisely as closed preserves all around a light and free space wherein perhaps

---

34. Metaphysically spoken; we cannot achieve anything by leaping [*er-springen*]. We are only able to find something in a search of an essentially different kind.

something unsaid might make an address without showing itself.

There is a conversation about painting that discusses to what extent what is painted in color only contains a sketch and outline of the image that it forms, but is supposed to contain these in such a manner that the sketch in the image does not properly show itself. In this conversation Cézanne says:

"One must not take people by the sleeve."[35]

35. ⟨Presumably Heidegger's own free translation, aiming at something adage-like from the following expression of Cézanne's: *"Personne ne me touchera [. . .] ne me mettra le grappin dessus. Jamais! Jamais!"*⟩ Cf. Emile Bernard, "Souvenirs sur Paul Cézanne," *Mercure de France* 69 (October 16, 1907): 606–27, 610. Emile Bernard, "Souvenirs sur Paul Cézanne (*Mercure de France*)," in *Conversations avec Cézanne*, ed. P.-M. Doran (Paris: Editions Macula, 1978), 49–80, 70. English translation: "No one is allowed to touch me . . . no one will get their claws into me! Never! Never!" in "Memories of Paul Cézanne (*Mercure de France*)," in *Conversations with Cézanne*, ed. Michael Doran, trans. Julie Lawrence Cochran (Berkeley: University of California Press, 2001), 50–79, 70.

Editor's Afterword

The present volume 79 contains the complete version of the Bremen lecture cycle *Insight Into That Which Is* from the year 1949 and the Freiburg lecture cycle *Basic Principles of Thinking* from the year 1957. Both lecture cycles, at the time of their oral delivery and subsequent partial publication (see below), provided to a broader public for the first time an insight—even if a still-limited one—into the beyng-historical thinking of the late Heidegger and therefore received a corresponding attentiveness. The "Bremen Lectures" document at the same time Heidegger's first public emergence after the Second World War.

Heidegger held the lecture cycle *Insight Into That Which Is* on December 1, 1949, in the Bremen Club and repeated it on March 25 and 26, 1950, at Bühlerhöhe. The four lectures are titled "The Thing," "Positionality," "The Danger," "The Turn." Heidegger also gave the first lecture, "The Thing," in a slightly expanded form under the title "Concerning the Thing" at the Bavarian Academy of Fine Arts in Munich on June 6, 1950. The first publication followed in 1954 in the anthology *Vorträge und Aufsätze*.[1] Part of the second lecture, "Positionality," served as the foundation for the otherwise entirely newly formulated

---

1. Martin Heidegger, "Das Ding," in *Vorträge und Aufsätze* (Stuttgart: Verlag Günther Neske, 1954), 163–81. Translator's Note: The lecture "The Thing" was first published in the first installment of the Bavarian Academy of Fine Art's yearbook *Gestalt und Gedanke* in 1951, where the title is already "The Thing." See Martin Heidegger, "Das Ding," in *Gestalt und Gedanke,* vol. 1, ed. Bayerischen Akademie der Schönen Künste (Munich: R. Oldenbourg, 1951), 128–48.

and expanded lecture "The Question Concerning Technology," which Heidegger held on November 18, 1953, in a series titled "The Arts in a Technological Age" hosted by said academy, and which was published in 1954 in volume three of the yearbook of this academy.[2] Further publication followed in the same year in *Vorträge und Aufsätze* and then in 1962 in *Die Technik und die Kehre*.[3] The third lecture, "The Danger," was never repeated outside of the lecture cycle and remained unpublished. Nonetheless, it was repeatedly cited without authorization in the secondary literature from available circulating transcripts. The fourth lecture, "The Turn," was published in 1962 in *Die Technik und die Kehre*, following the version lectured.[4]

The first transcription of the "Bremen Lectures," which does not yet contain the partitioning into four lectures, Heidegger noted as from October 1949 at the hut. The first (handwritten) fair copy, which contains the above-mentioned subdivision, followed in Freiburg and Meßkirch in November 1949, and a second fair copy, likewise handwritten, in March 1950. In this last copy, the first seven paragraphs of the thing lecture are separated out and affixed at the head of the whole lecture cycle under the title "The Point of Reference."

The text present here is oriented to the second handwritten fair copy of Heidegger's and the two typescripts prepared from this that were overseen by Heidegger and provided with marginal notes. The marginal notes are reproduced in the printed text by notes indicated with lowercase letters.[5] Of the fourth lecture, "The Turn," only one typescript was present in addition to the handwritten text. The handwritten transcript and

---

2. Martin Heidegger, "Die Frage nach der Technik," in *Gestalt und Gedanke*, vol. 3: *Die Künste im technischen Zeitalter*, ed. Bayerischen Akademie der Schönen Künste (Munich: R. Oldenbourg, 1954), 70–108.

3. Martin Heidegger, "Die Frage nach der Technik," in *Vorträge und Aufsätze* (Stuttgart: Verlag Günther Neske, 1954), 13–44, and in *Die Technik und die Kehre, Opuscula*, vol. 1 (Pfullingen: Verlag Günther Neske, 1962), 5–36.

4. Martin Heidegger, "Die Kehre," in *Die Technik und die Kehre, Opuscula*, vol. 1 (Pfullingen: Verlag Günther Neske, 1962), 37–47.

5. Translator's Note: This system of enumeration has not been adhered to in the present translation. See the "Translator's Foreword" above (xv) for details.

the typescript were collated by the editor with minor transcription errors corrected.

For the lecture "The Thing," an appendix to manuscript p. 9 (cf. p. 11, marginal note a) and a few not fully formulated sketches to this lecture (cf. p. 22f.) are adjoined.[6] The fourth lecture, "The Turn," in the version here presented is nearly identical to the already published version. In two places, the latter provides a sentence or a phrase more, respectively (cf. *Opuscula* 1, pp. 44 and 46).[7]

* * *

Heidegger held the five "Freiburg Lectures," which form the second part of volume 79, in the summer semester of 1957 under the title *Basic Principles of Thinking*, in the context of the *studium generale* at the University of Freiburg.

The first lecture of this cycle Heidegger published under the title of the cycle as a whole, "Principles of Thinking," in a revised form in the Festschrift for Victor v. Gebsattel in the *Jahrbuch für Psychologie und Psychotherapie*, vol. 6, issues 1–3, 1958, pp. 33–41. The third and most famous lecture of this cycle was held by Heidegger under the title "The Principle of Identity" as a ceremonial address for the anniversary celebration of the Albert-Ludwig University Freiburg on its five-hundred-year anniversary on June 27, 1957, in the Freiburger Stadthalle. The lecture was published in the first volume of the four-volume Festschrift for Albert Ludwig University on pages 69–79.[8] In the same year, the

---

6. Translator's Note: see above, 10 n. 1 and 21–22.

7. Translator's Note: Martin Heidegger, "Die Kehre," now in *Identität und Differenz*, ed. Friedrich-Wilhelm von Herrmann, *Gesamtausgabe* vol. 11 (Frankfurt am Main: Vittorio Klostermann, 2006), 113–24. The additions in question are to GA 79: 74/70, paragraph ending "Flashing entry is the event of appropriation in beyng itself," where GA 11: 121 adds the sentence: "The event of appropriation [*Ereignis*] is an appropriative eyeing [*eignende Eräugnis*]" and to GA 79: 76/72, paragraph ending "Yet no historiological conception of history as occurrence brings in the fitting [*schicklichen*] relation to destiny," where GA 11: 123 continues this sentence with "and nothing of its essential place of origin in the event of the truth of being."

8. Translator's Note: Martin Heidegger, "Der Satz der Identität," in *Die Albert-Ludwigs-Universität Freiburg 1457–1957: Die Festvorträge bei der*

lecture appeared unaltered in the volume *Identity and Difference* in the Neske-Verlag, Pfullingen.[9] The second, fourth, and fifth lectures of the Freiburg lecture cycle remained unpublished.

As with the "Bremen Lectures," it is also the case with the "Freiburg Lectures" that the manuscript and transcripts overseen by Heidegger himself—with one exception—form the basis for the text presented here. The manuscript and transcripts were collated by the editor, the marginal comments in the manuscript adopted as marginalia in the printed text. Nevertheless, the manuscript of the third lecture, "The Principle of Identity," is missing. The textual basis for the publication of this lecture is consequently the typewritten transcript of the manuscript heavily revised by Heidegger. For the fifth lecture, a second typewritten transcript contains numerous additional textual improvements in Heidegger's hand, which are indicated by the editor in the marginalia with a special notation.

In all the texts present in this volume, Heidegger's characteristic manner of writing was retained even when it contravened or diverged from pertinent writing conventions. The latter concerns in particular the manner of writing "being/beyng," which was not standardized to "being," as was the case in the texts already published. The term *"Ge-Stell"* [positionality] forms the sole exception, which predominates in this way of writing exclusively, as distinct from the current concept of frameworks [*Gestells*]. The punctuation was slightly amended. The citations were—as far as possible—verified in Heidegger's personal copies and the bibliographical references in the text occurring only in abbreviation were added or expanded in the footnotes.

*   *   *

Under the title *Insight Into That Which Is* and following the guiding thread of the question concerning the full essence of the thing and its unguarding in the age of technology as the dominance of "positionality," in which beings still appear only in the form of orderable standing reserve, the "Bremen

---

Jubiläumsfeier (Freiburg im Breisgau: Hans Ferdinand Schulz Verlag, 1957), 69–79.

9. Martin Heidegger, *Identität und Differenz* (Pfullingen: Günther Neske Verlag, 1957).

Lectures" unfold the essential question concerning the fundamental occurrence of this beyng-historical constellation and
the danger concealed in it along with its possible overcoming.
The authentic danger, according to Heidegger, lies in the complete burial of the occurrence of the unconcealment of beings,
which, in the epochal historical interplay of disclosure and
concealment, of clearing and concealment of beyng, has its
place in the event of appropriation.

As an attempt to experience thinking from out of its basic
principles, the "Freiburg Lectures" run the historical risk of entering into the world-historical undecidedness of thinking and,
in the conflict of thinking with that from where it is called, of
thinking that which it thinks and thereby of thinking how it
thinks. This attempt scrutinizes the basic principles of thinking,
conventionally so called—such as the principles of identity, of
contradiction, and of reason—in a tradition of thinking that releases us for another appropriation and thus makes possible a
transformation of the thinking that dominates our age. It in-
quires back into the place of origin of the laws of thought, where
no science reaches, i.e., into that other region of the location of
the identity of thinking and being and thus into that other identity as belonging together, which essences as the taking into
ownership of both the human and of being by the event of the
clearing of beyng.

*   *   *

I thank the executor of the surviving papers, Dr. Hermann
Heidegger, for the trust bestowed in the assignment of the editorial work on this volume. I am indebted to Prof. Dr. Friedrich-Wilhelm von Herrmann and Dr. Hartmut Tietjen for numerous suggestions and references for the textual and formal
configuration of this volume. Doctoral candidate Mark Mi-
chalski and Dr. Hartmut Tietjen deserve my thanks for their
support in the search for citation references and the expan-
sion of the bibliographical information. The reference to Cézanne's statement I owe to Prof. François Fédier (Paris). For
their care in the reading of the corrections, I thank Peter
Krumhold and again Dr. Hartmut Tietjen.

Düsseldorf, May 1994   Petra Jaeger

GERMAN-ENGLISH GLOSSARY

Abgrund	abyss
absetzen	to set apart, to set aside
absperren	to isolate
abspringen	to leap away, to depart
Absprung	leap of departure, leap that departs
Abstand	distance
Abständige	what stands at a distance
Abstandlose	distanceless
Abstehen	distancing
abstellen	to assign
Aktuelle	the current, current events
an-sprechen	to speak to
Anblick	sighting
anblicken	to sight
andauern	to last
andenken	to commemorate, to thoughtfully remember
anfänglich	inceptual, inceptually
anfordern	to commandeer
Angang	concerned approach
angehen	to concernfully approach
Angehende	what concernfully approaches
Ankunft	arrival, arriving
Ansehen	regarding
Ansicht	aspect
ansprechen	to address
Anspruch	claim
Anstehen	subsistence

anstehende	subsisting
Anwesen	presence
Anwesende	what presences, that which presences
Apparate	apparatus, trappings
Apparaturen	devices
auf der Stelle zur Stelle	in place and at the ready
aufblitzen	to flash up
aufhalten (sich)	to reside
aufstellen	to set up
ausbleiben	to remain outstanding, to exclude
auslegen	to interpret
Aussage	expression, utterance, statement
Aussehen	outward appearance, outward appearing
bedenken	to consider
Bedrängnis	plight
befreien	to release, liberate
befremdlich	bewildering
begründen	to found
beistellen	to position alongside
Bereich	realm
bergen	to shelter, harbor
Bergung	sheltering
berückend	charming
beseitigen	to abolish
Besinnung	pondering, meditation
Bestand	standing reserve, inventory, stock; persistency
beständig	constant
Beständige	something constant
beständigen	to make constant
Beständigkeit	constancy
Beständigung	constancy
Bestandsicherung	securing of status
Bestandstücke	piece of inventory
bestehen	to consist, persist, subsist
Bestellen	requisitioning

bestellen	to order; *ein Acker, Feld bestellen:* to tend a field
Bestellung	ordering
bestrickend	captivating
Betreiben	pursuits, pursuing
betreiben	to pursue, conduct
Betriebe	industry
bezaubernd	enchanting
Bezirk	domain
Blick	glance, view
blicken	to glance, to look
Blitzen	the lightning flash
blitzen	to flash
Boden	soil, floor, footing
Bodenlosigkeit	uprootedness from the soil
Bodenständigkeit	rootedness in the soil
Bürgschaft	guarantee
darlegen	to exposit, to expose
Darlegung	exposition
denken	to think
Denkmaschine	thinking machine
Differenz	difference
Dinge und Wesen	things and beings
Distanz	longinquity
doppeldeutig	double meaning
Doppeldeutigkeit	dual meaning
Drangsal	tribulation
durchsagen	talking through
durchwalten	to pervade
eigen	to own
eigens	properly
eigentlich	authentic, genuine
Eigentum	propriety
eignen (sich)	to be proper to
einbehalten	to retain, include
einbestellen	arrange into, order into
Einblick	insight
Einblitz	flashing entry
Eindeutigkeit	univocality
Einfach	simplistic, simple

Einfalt	single fold
einfältig	simple
einig	united, unified
Einigende	what unites
Einkehr	entrance
einkehren	to enter, to turn to enter
einrichten (sich)	to install (oneself)
Einsicht	inspection
einspannen	to load into
einsperren	to confine in
einstellen	to insert
entschicken	to dispense
Ent-setzen	displacement
Entbergung	disclosure
entfallen	to lapse (into)
Entfernung	distance, remoteness
entgegensetzen	to set against
Entgegensetzung	contrariety
entgegenstehen	stand across from
Entrückende	carrying away
entsetzen	to oust, to displace
Entsetzende	the horrible, horrifying
Entsetzliche	the horrifying
entziehen	to withdraw
Entzückende	pulling back
erblicken	to catch sight of
Erblickte	what is caught sight of
ereignen	to appropriate
ereignen (sich)	to take place
ereignend	appropriating, appropriatingly
Ereignis	event, the event of appropriation, appropriative event
erfahren	to experience; to find out
Erfolg	success
Erläuterung	elucidation
erörtern	to discuss; to situate
Fährnis	peril
Ferne	the far off, far away, the remote
festlegen	to establish

fördern	to conduct, to further
Formel	formula, formulation
fortreißen	to wrest away
Fortriß	wresting away
Freie	the space of freedom
freigeben	to release
freilassen	to release, let free
freisetzen	to release
Fug	joint
fügen (sich)	to join; to comply with
fügsam	pliant
Ge-Stell	positionality
Gebiet	region
Gebirg	refuge
geborgen	hidden
Gefahr	danger
gefahrlos	dangerless
Gefäß	vessel
Gefüge	jointure
Gegen-wart	impending
Gegenblick	counter gaze
Gegensatz	antagonism; opposition
Gegenstand	object
Gegenständige	the oppositional object, what is oppositionally objective
Gegenständlichkeit	objectivity
Gegenstehen	objective stance
Gegenüber	opposition
gegenüber	over against
Gegenüberstehen	standing opposite
Gegenwart	present
Gelassenheit	releasement
Gepräge	cast, stamping, impression
Geraff	plundering
Gering	circling; the slight
gering	slight
gesammelt	gathered, collected, concentrated, cumulative
geschehen	to occur
Geschichte	history

Geschick	dispensation, destiny
geschickhafte	dispensationally
Geschickliche	what is dispensational
Geschiebe	commotion, pistons
Gesetztheit	positedness
Gestänge	scaffolding, rod assemblies
Gestelle	framework
Gestelltheit	positionhood
Gestellung	conscription, conscripting
Getriebe	drive; gearing
getrübt	murky
Geviert	the fourfold
gewähren	to afford, grant, warrant
Gewährte	what is granted
Gewesene	what has-been
gleich	equal, equivalent
Gleich-Giltige	what is of equal value, the equivalent
Gleich-Gültige	the indifferent
Gleiche	the equal, the equivalent; equality
Grund	ground, basis
Grund-Satz	grounding principle, grounding statement
Grundbestand	fundamental standing reserve
Grundsatz	basic principle
grundsätzliche	fundamental
Grundton	tonic pitch
Gunst	grace
Guss	the pour
Haltung	bearing
Heimatlosigkeit	lack of homeland
Heimische	the homely
herausfordern	to challenge (forth), to provoke
herausfördern	to expedite (along)
heraussetzen	to transpose something outside something
Hereinwähren	continuing
Herkunft	provenance, place of origin
Herrschaft	dominance

herrschen	to master, to dominate, to preside, predominate
Herstand	what stands here
herstehen	to stand here
herstellen	to produce
Herwähren	enduring
Hinblick	regard; look to
Hinsicht	vantage, respect
hinstellen	to poise
Historie	historiology
historisch	historiological, historiologically
Huld	favor
hüten	to protect
Identische	the identical
Insichstehen	standing-on-its-own
jäh	suddenly
Kehre	the turn
kehren	to turn
Kreisgang	circuit
Lautere	limpid
Leere	the empty, emptiness
legen	to lay
Leiden	suffering
Leidenschaft	passion
leuchten	to illuminate
Lichtblick	glimmer
lichten	to light up
lichtend	lighting, clearing
Lichtung	illuminated clearing
Mär	fable
Märchen	fairy tale
Märchenhafte	the fabulous
Maß	measure
Maßgabe	standard, rule, stipulation
maßgebende	standard, authoritative, standard setting
meditieren	to meditate
Mehrdeutigkeit	equivocality
Nachdenken	contemplation, retrospective thinking

nachdenken	to contemplate
nachsetzen	to set after
nachsinnen	to ponder, meditate
nachstellen	to pursue
Nähe	nearness; *in der Nähe:* in the vicinity
nähern	to bring near
Obhut	protection
Ort	place
Ortschaft	locality, location
prägen	to stamp, cast, impress
preisgeben	to relinquish
raffen	to reap
Ratlose	the clueless
Ratsal	counsel
Rede	talk
reden	to talk
Reigen	round dance
reißen	to rend, to wrest
Ring	the ring
ring	nimble; scant
Ringe	the nimble, nimbleness; pliancy
Riß	rift
Rückbeziehung	return relation, relation back to itself
Rundfunkrat	the public broadcast advisory council
Sache	issue at stake, affair, matter
Sage	saying; legend
sagen	to say
Sagenhafte	the legendary
Satz	principle, proposition, statement
schicken	to send
schicken (sich)	to send (oneself); to be fitting, suitable; to comply
schicklichen	fateful
Schicksal	fate
Schickung	sending

schlechthin	plain and simple, just, unqualifiedly
schmiegsam	supple
schonen	to protect
Schweben	suspension
schweben	to be suspended, to hover
Schwingen	resonance
schwingen	to resonate
seiend	extant
Seiende	the being
Sein	being
Seinlassen	letting be
Seinsvergessenheit	forgetfulness of being, forgetting of being
Selbe	the same
Selbststand	self-standing
Selbständiges	something independent
setzen	to posit, to set
Seyn	beyng
Spende	donation
spenden	to donate
Spiegel-Spiel	mirror-play
Sprache	language, speech
sprechen	to speak
Spruch	pronouncement
Sprung	leap
spüren	to detect
Stand	standing, stance, status
Ständige	something steady
Ständigkeit	steadiness
Stätte	site
Steg	route
steil	abruptly
Stelle	place
stellen	to place, to set, to position, to pose
stellen (auf)	to impose upon (for)
stetig	constant, steady
stillen	to appease
Strecke	interval

Streit	discord, strife
Streitfall	(discordant) dispute
Trägheit	inertia
Trank	oblation
Treiben	impulse, ambition
Treibstoff	propellant
trennen	to sunder
Triebkraft	propulsion
Trunk	libation
Tun und Lassen	doing and allowing
übereignen	to transfer into the ownership of . . .
überlegen	to ponder
Überlieferung	tradition
übermäßig	immeasurably
überreichen	to reach over, give over
Umtrieb	bustle
ungefährlich	innocuous
Ungefährliche	the innocuous
unscheinbar	inapparent, inconspicuous
Unterkunft	accommodation
Unterschied	differentiation
unterstellen	to subordinate, place under
ursprünglich	originary
Verbergung	harboring
verborgen	concealed, hidden
verbürgen	to guarantee
vereignen	to bring into ownership
Vereignung	bringing into ownership
verfallen	to deteriorate, to fall for
Vergangene	the past
Vergegenwärtigung	making present
Vergessenheit	forgetting, forgetfulness
verhalten	reserved
verhalten	to comport; to relate
Verhältnismäßige	the relational
Verhängnis	disaster
Verödung	devastation
Versammlung	collection, gathering
verschwenden	to squander

versprechen	to promise
verstellen	to dissemble, disguise
verwahren	to preserve
Verwahrlosung	unguarding
verwehren	to prohibit
verweigern	to refuse, deny
Verweigerung	refusal, denial
verweilen	to linger; to let abide
verwenden	to turn about; to use, apply
verwinden	to convert
Verwindung	conversion
verzaubern	to bewitch
Vierung	fouring
Vollendung	completion
Vordenken	thinking ahead
vorenthalten	to withhold
Vorfall	incident
vorfallen	to befall
Vorkommnis	incident
vorstellen	to represent, to conceive
Vorstellung	representation, conception
vorwaltende	presiding
Wachsamkeit	vigilance
Wahr	guard
wahren	to guard
Währen	perseverance, enduring
währen	to endure, persevere
Währende	what endures
Wahrnis	guardian, guardianship
walten	to hold sway, to reign
Wandlung	alteration
Wechselbezug	reciprocal relation
wegsetzen	to move away
Weile	while, duration
weilen	to abide
Weiliges	that which abides
Weisung	directive
wenden (sich)	to turn about
wirkfähig	effective
Wirkliches	something actual

Wirksame	the effectual
Wirksamkeit	effectiveness
zaubern	to conjure
zeigen	to show, reveal
Zerrissenheit	tearing
ziehen	to draw
zücken	to pull out
zueignen	to deliver into ownership
Zueinander	reciprocality
Zumutung	imposition
Zuordnung	coordination
zusagen	to accord
Zusammen	togetherness, the together
Zusammengehörigkeit	belonging-together
zusammenlegen	to lay together
zusetzen	to importune upon
zuspielen	to playfully solicit
zusprechen	avow
Zuspruch	appeal
zutrauen	to entrust, to betroth
Zweideutigkeit	ambiguity

ENGLISH-GERMAN GLOSSARY

abide	*weilen*
abolish	*beseitigen*
abruptly	*steil*
abyss	*Abgrund*
accommodation	*Unterkunft*
accord	*zusagen*
actual, what is	*Wirkliches*
address	*ansprechen*
affair	*Sache*
afford	*gewähren*
alteration	*Wandlung*
ambiguity	*Zweideutigkeit*
ambition	*Treiben*
antagonism	*Gegensatz*
apparatus	*Apparate*
appeal	*Zuspruch*
appease	*stillen*
appropriate	*ereignen*
appropriating, appropriatingly	*ereignend*
appropriative event	*Ereignis*
arrange into	*einbestellen*
arrival, arriving	*Ankunft*
aspect	*Ansicht*
assign	*abstellen*
authentic	*eigentlich*
authoritative	*Maßgabe*
avow	*zusprechen*
basic principle	*Grundsatz*
basis	*Grund*

to be fitting	*schicken (sich)*
be proper to	*eignen (sich)*
be suitable	*schicken (sich)*
bearing	*Haltung*
befall	*vorfallen*
being	*Sein*
being (a, the)	*Seiende*
belonging-together	*Zusammengehörigkeit*
betroth	*zutrauen*
bewildering	*befremdlich*
bewitch	*verzaubern*
beyng	*Seyn*
bring into ownership	*vereignen*
bring near	*nähern*
bringing into ownership	*Vereignung*
bustle	*Umtrieb*
captivating	*bestrickend*
carrying away	*Entrückende*
cast	*Gepräge*
to cast	*prägen*
catch sight of	*erblicken*
caught sight of, what is	*Erblickte*
challenge (forth)	*herausfordern*
charming	*berückend*
circling	*Gering*
circuit	*Kreisgang*
claim	*Anspruch*
clearing	*lichtend*
clueless	*Ratlose*
collected	*gesammelt*
collection	*Versammlung*
commandeer	*anfordern*
commemorate	*andenken*
commotion	*Geschiebe*
completion	*Vollendung*
comply with	*fügen (sich); schicken (sich)*
comport	*verhalten*
concealed	*verborgen*
conceive	*vorstellen*
concentrated	*gesammelt*

conception	*Vorstellung*
concerned approach	*Angang*
concernfully approach	*angehen*
concernfully approaches, what	*Angehende*
conduct	*fördern*
confine in	*einsperren*
conjure	*zaubern*
conscription, conscripting	*Gestellung*
consider	*bedenken*
consist	*bestehen*
constancy	*Beständigkeit, Beständigung*
constant	*beständig, stetig*
constant, what is	*Beständige*
contemplate	*nachdenken*
contemplation	*Nachdenken*
continuing	*Hereinwähren*
contrariety	*Entgegensetzung*
conversion	*Verwindung*
convert	*verwinden*
coordination	*Zuordnung*
counsel	*Ratsal*
countergaze	*Gegenblick*
cumulative	*gesammelt*
current, current events	*Aktuelle*
danger	*Gefahr*
dangerless	*gefahrlos*
deliver into ownership	*zueignen*
denial	*Verweigerung*
deny	*verweigern*
depart	*abspringen*
destiny	*Geschick*
detect	*spüren*
deteriorate	*verfallen*
devastation	*Verödung*
devices	*Apparaturen*
difference	*Differenz*
differentiation	*Unterschied*
directive	*Weisung*
disaster	*Verhängnis*
disclosure	*Entbergung*

discord	*Streit*
discuss	*erörtern*
disguise	*verstellen*
dispensation	*Geschichte*
dispensational, what is	*Geschickliche*
dispensationally	*geschickhafte*
dispense	*entschicken*
displace	*entsetzen*
displacement	*Ent-setzen*
dispute (discordant)	*Streitfall*
dissemble	*verstellen*
distance	*Abstand, Entfernung*
distanceless	*Abstandlose*
distancing	*Abstehen*
doing and allowing	*Tun und Lassen*
domain	*Bezirk*
dominance	*Herrschaft*
dominate	*herrschen*
donate	*spenden*
donation	*Spende*
double meaning	*doppeldeutig*
draw	*ziehen*
drive	*Getriebe*
drive for	*betreiben*
dual meaning	*Doppeldeutigkeit*
the easy, ease	*Ringe*
effective	*wirkfähig*
effectiveness	*Wirksamkeit*
effectual	*Wirksame*
elucidation	*Erläuterung*
the empty, emptiness	*Leere*
enchanting	*bezaubernd*
endure	*währen*
what endures	*Währende*
enduring	*Herwähren, Währen*
enter	*einkehren*
entrance	*Einkehr*
entrust	*zutrauen*
equal, equivalent	*gleich*
equal, equivalent; equality	*Gleiche*

equivalent, what is of equal value	*Gleich-Giltige*
equivocality	*Mehrdeutigkeit*
establish	*festlegen*
event, event of appropriation	*Ereignis*
exclude	*ausbleiben*
expedite (along)	*herausfördern*
experience	*erfahren*
expose	*darlegen*
exposit	*darlegen*
exposition	*Darlegung*
expression	*Aussage*
extant	*seiend*
fable	*Mär*
fabulous	*Märchenhafte*
fairy tale	*Märchen*
fall for	*verfallen*
far off, far away	*Ferne*
fate	*Schicksal*
fateful	*schicklichen*
favor	*Huld*
find out	*erfahren*
flash	*blitzen*
flash up	*aufblitzen*
flashing entry	*Einblitz*
floor	*Boden*
footing	*Boden*
forgetfulness of being, forgetting of being	*Seinsvergessenheit*
forgetting, forgetfulness	*Vergessenheit*
formula, formulation	*Formel*
found	*begründen*
fouring	*Vierung*
fourfold	*Geviert*
framework	*Gestelle*
fundamental	*grundsätzliche*
fundamental standing reserve	*Grundbestand*
further	*fördern*
gathered	*gesammelt*
gathering	*Versammlung*

gearing	*Getriebe*
genuine	*eigentlich*
give over	*überreichen*
glance	*Blick*
to glance	*blicken*
glimmer	*Lichtblick*
grace	*Gunst*
grant	*gewähren*
granted, what is	*Gewährte*
ground	*Grund*
grounding principle	*Grund-Satz*
grounding statement	*Grund-Satz*
guarantee	*Bürgschaft*
to guarantee	*verbürgen*
guard	*Wahr*
to guard	*wahren*
guardian, guardianship	*Wahrnis*
harbor	*bergen*
harboring	*Verbergung*
has-been	*Gewesene*
hidden	*geborgen, verborgen*
historiological, historiologically	*historisch*
historiology	*Historie*
history	*Geschichte*
hold sway	*walten*
homely	*Heimische*
horrible	*Entsetzende*
horrifying	*Entsetzende, Entsetzliche*
identical	*Identische*
illuminate	*leuchten*
illuminated clearing	*Lichtung*
immeasurably	*übermäßig*
impending	*Gegen-wart*
importune upon	*zusetzen*
impose upon (for)	*stellen (auf)*
imposition	*Zumutung*
impress	*prägen*
impression	*Gepräge*
impulse	*Treiben*

included	*einbehalten*
in place and at the ready	*auf der Stelle zur Stelle*
in the vicinity	*in der Nähe*
inapparent	*unscheinbar*
inceptual, inceptually	*anfänglich*
incident	*Vorfall, Vorkommnis*
inconspicuous	*unauffällig; unscheinbar*
independent, what is	*Selbständiges*
indifferent	*Gleich-Gültige*
industry	*Betriebe*
inertia	*Trägheit*
innocuous	*ungefährlich*
insert	*einstellen*
insight	*Einblick*
inspection	*Einsicht*
install (oneself)	*einrichten sich*
interpret	*auslegen*
interval	*Strecke*
inventory	*Bestand*
isolate	*absperren*
issue at stake	*Sache*
join	*fügen (sich)*
joint	*Fug*
jointure	*Gefüge*
just	*schlechthin*
lack of homeland	*Heimatlosigkeit*
language	*Sprache*
lapse (into)	*entfallen*
last	*andauern*
lay	*legen*
lay together	*zusammenlegen*
leap	*Sprung*
leap away	*abspringen*
leap of departure, leap that departs	*Absprung*
legend	*Sage*
legendary	*Sagenhafte*
let abide	*verweilen*
letting be	*Seinlassen*
libation	*Trunk*

liberate	*befreien*
light up	*lichten*
lighting	*lichtend*
lightning flash	*Blitzen*
limpid	*Lautere*
linger	*verweilen*
load into	*einspannen*
locality, location	*Ortschaft*
longinquity	*Distanz*
look	*blicken*
look to	*Hinblick*
make constant	*beständigen*
making present	*Vergegenwärtigung*
master	*herrschen*
matter	*Sache*
measure	*Maß*
meditate	*meditieren, nachsinnen*
meditation	*Besinnung*
mirror-play	*Spiegel-Spiel*
move away	*wegsetzen*
murky	*getrübt*
nearness	*Nähe*
nimble	*ring; Ringe*
object	*Gegenstand*
objective stance	*Gegenstehen*
objectivity	*Gegenständlichkeit*
oblation	*Trank*
occur	*geschehen*
opposition	*Gegensatz; Gegenüber*
oppositional object	*Gegenständige*
oppositionally objective	*Gegenständige*
order	*bestellen*
order into	*einbestellen*
ordering	*Bestellung*
originary	*ursprünglich*
oust	*entsetzen*
outward appearance, outward appearing	*Aussehen*
over against	*gegenüber*
own	*eigen*

passion	*Leidenschaft*
past	*Vergangene*
peril	*Fährnis*
perseverance	*Währen*
persevere	*währen*
persist	*bestehen*
persistency	*Bestand*
pervade	*durchwalten*
piece of inventory	*Bestandstücke*
pistons	*Geschiebe*
place	*Ort; Stelle*
to place	*stellen*
place of origin	*Herkunft*
place under	*unterstellen*
plain and simple	*schlechthin*
playfully solicit	*zuspielen*
pliancy	*Fügsame; Ringe*
pliant	*fügsam*
plight	*Bedrängnis*
plundering	*Geraff*
poise	*hinstellen*
ponder	*nachsinnen, überlegen*
pondering	*Besinnung*
pose	*stellen*
posit	*setzen*
positedness	*Gesetzit*
position	*stellen*
position alongside	*beistellen*
positionality	*Ge-Stell*
positionhood	*Gestellit*
pour	*Guss*
predominate	*herrschen*
presence	*Anwesen*
presences, that which presences	*Anwesende*
present	*Gegenwart*
preserve	*verwahren*
preside	*herrschen*
presiding	*vorwaltende*
principle	*Satz*

produce	*herstellen*
prohibit	*verwehren*
promise	*versprechen*
pronouncement	*Spruch*
propellant	*Treibstoff*
properly	*eigens*
proposition	*Satz*
propriety	*Eigentum*
propulsion	*Triebkraft*
protect	*hüten, schonen*
protection	*Obhut*
provenance	*Herkunft*
public broadcast advisory council	*Rundfunkrat*
pull out	*zücken*
pulling back	*Entzückende*
pursue	*nachstellen; betreiben*
pursuits, pursuing	*Betreiben*
reach over	*überreichen*
realm	*Bereich*
reap	*raffen*
reciprocal relation	*Wechselbezug*
reciprocality	*Zueinander*
refuge	*Gebirg*
refusal	*Verweigerung*
refuse	*verweigern*
regard	*Hinblick*
regarding	*Ansehen*
region	*Gebiet*
reign	*walten*
relate	*verhalten*
relation back to itself	*Rückbeziehung*
relational	*Verhältnismäßige*
release	*befreien, freigeben, freilassen, freisetzen*
releasement	*Gelassenheit*
relinquish	*preisgeben*
remain outstanding	*ausbleiben*
remote	*Ferne*
remoteness	*Entfernung*

rend	*reißen*
represent	*vorstellen*
representation	*Vorstellung*
requisitioning	*Bestellen*
reserved	*verhalten*
reside	*aufhalten (sich)*
resonance	*Schwingen*
resonate	*schwingen*
respect	*Hinsicht*
retain	*einbehalten*
retrospective thinking	*Nachdenken*
return relation	*Rückbeziehung*
reveal	*zeigen*
rift	*Riß*
ring	*Ring*
rod assemblies	*Gestänge*
rootedness in the soil	*Bodenständigkeit*
round dance	*Reigen*
route	*Steg*
rule	*Maß*
same	*Selbe*
say	*sagen*
saying	*Sage*
scaffolding	*Gestänge*
scant	*ring*
securing of status	*Bestandsicherung*
self-standing	*Selbststand*
send	*schicken*
sending	*Schickung*
set	*setzen; stellen*
set after	*nachsetzen*
set against	*entgegensetzen*
set apart	*absetzen*
set aside	*absetzen*
set up	*aufstellen*
shelter	*bergen*
sheltering	*Bergung*
show	*zeigen*
sight	*anblicken*
sighting	*Anblick*

simple	*einfältig*
simplistic, simple	*Einfach*
single fold	*Einfalt*
site	*Stätte*
situate	*erörtern*
slight	*gering*
the slight	*Gering*
soil	*Boden*
space of freedom	*Freie*
speak	*sprechen*
speak to	*an-sprechen*
speech	*Sprache*
squander	*verschwenden*
stamp	*prägen*
stamping	*Gepräge*
stance	*Stand*
stand across from	*entgegenstehen*
stand here	*herstehen*
standard	*Maß, Maßgabe*
standard setting	*maßgebende*
standing	*Stand*
standing opposite	*Gegenüberstehen*
standing reserve	*Bestand*
standing-on-its-own	*Insichstehen*
stands at a distance, what	*Abständige*
stands here, what	*Herstand*
statement	*Aussage; Satz*
status	*Stand*
steadiness	*Ständigkeit*
steady, what is	*Ständige*
stipulation	*Maßgabe*
stock	*Bestand*
strife	*Streit*
subordinate	*unterstellen*
subsist	*bestehen*
subsistence	*Anstehen*
subsisting	*anstehende*
success	*Erfolg*
suddenly	*jäh*
suffering	*Leiden*

sunder	*trennen*
supple	*schmiegsam*
to be suspended	*schweben*
suspension	*Schweben*
take place	*ereignen sich*
talk	*Rede*
to talk	*reden*
talking through	*durchsagen*
tearing	*Zerrissenheit*
tend a field	*ein Acker bestellen*
things and beings	*Dinge und Wesen*
think	*denken*
thinking ahead	*Vordenken*
thinking machine	*Denkmaschine*
thoughtfully remember	*andenken*
togetherness, together	*Zusammen*
tonic pitch	*Grundton*
tradition	*Überlieferung*
transfer into the	*übereignen*
ownership of . . .	
transpose something	*heraussetzen*
outside something	
trappings	*Apparate*
tribulation	*Drangsal*
turn	*Kehre*
to turn	*kehren*
turn about	*verwenden; wenden (sich)*
unguarding	*Verwahrlosung*
unified	*einig*
united	*einig*
unites, what	*Einigende*
univocality	*Eindeutigkeit*
uprootedness from the soil	*Bodenlosigkeit*
utterance	*Aussage*
vantage	*Hinsicht*
vessel	*Gefäß*
view	*Blick*
vigilance	*Wachsamkeit*
warrant	*gewähren*
while	*Weile*

whiling	*Weiliges*
withdraw	*entziehen*
withhold	*vorenthalten*
wrest	*reißen*
wrest away	*fortreißen*
wresting away	*Fortriß*